P9-CRB-785

Diabetes 101

Diabetes 101

A Pure and Simple Guide for People Who Use Insulin

3rd Edition

Betty Page Brackenridge, MS, RD, CDE
Richard O. Dolinar, MD

JOHN WILEY & SONS, INC.

New York • Chichester • Weinheim • Brisbane • Singapore • Toronto

This third edition of *Diabetes 101* is dedicated with deep love and thanks to our respective families and loved ones who suffer through our busy schedules and love us anyway.

For Dr. Dolinar: My wife, Barbara, and sons, Mark and Ryan.

For Betty: David, Carrie, Connie, Brent, and Cris, all of whom make every day a joyful gift.

Special Note

Consult your doctor before making any change in your diabetes care plan. The information contained in this book can help you become more involved and informed regarding your diabetes management. But it is **not** a substitute for regular diabetes care by your physician or for personalized diabetes education.

Before You Begin

A lot of information is available to the person with diabetes. There are mountains of pamphlets, instruction sheets, and diet forms. There are rooms filled with films, slides, and tapes. There is a stream of committed health professionals gushing sometimes mind-numbing torrents of well-meaning words. And there are many books.

So why write another one? Great question. And we think we have a great answer. We wrote this little book because there is a need. Not a need for another *War and Peace* of diabetes. A need, rather, for a brief and readable guide to important basic information needed every day by people who take insulin to control their diabetes.

Some information about diabetes is vital to daily living. That information is in this book. Some additional liberating information about diabetes is also included.

But some things are **not** in this book because everything just can't be learned all at once. A lot of information about diabetes that is interesting—especially to doctors and nurses— but not necessary for daily diabetes care has been left out. And certain advanced skills have also been omitted. There are wonderful books that cover such topics in great detail. We encourage you to read them when you have the need. Today, though, read this little book.

We've been told it's helpful.

Betty Brackenridge
Richard Dolinar

Acknowledgments

This book carries the names of only two authors. In reality, many others have contributed greatly to its development and we thank them all for their help and encouragement. Our primary thanks must go to our patients. They have taught us about the reality of living with diabetes and, in that way, have shown us the difference between what they truly needed to know and what we thought they should know.

Dr. Dolinar extends special thanks to the outstanding group of physicians present at Duke University Medical Center in the early 1980s who had a major impact on his interest in and approach to diabetes. They include Harold Lebovitz, M.D., head of the Department of Endocrinology at that time; George Eisenbarth, M.D., Ph.D., who provided many unique insights regarding Type 1 diabetes; George "Jay" Ellis, M.D., who emphasized the importance of practical patient education and who modeled a dynamic problem-solving method of diabetes management, and Warner Burch, M.D., who contributed his practical approach to patient care. Harry McPherson, M.D., Frank Neelon, M.D., Jerome Feldman, M.D., Charles Johnson, M.D., Mark Feinglos, M.D., Marc Drezner, M.D., and Titus

Allen, M.D., were very kind to share their many clinical "pearls of wisdom." And thanks to Trish Hart, R.N., Donna Perry, and also to Mrs. Johnnie Alexander who provided unique support in their own very special ways.

Betty Brackenridge warmly acknowledges the many colleagues who have contributed to this latest version of *Diabetes 101* with their skillful advice and exceptional example, especially Kris Swenson, Virginia Valentine, Bob Anderson, and Richard Rubin. She also wishes to acknowledge the members of the American Association of Diabetes Educators who dedicate their love and skill to opening windows of freedom for those with diabetes.

Section One: The Basics

Chapter 1. The Journey: Are You My Doctor? 3

Chapter 2. Riding the Bicycle: An Overview 9

Chapter 3. Keeping the Fire Burning: Insulin 15

Chapter 4. Feeding the Flames: Nutrition 29

Chapter 5. Installing the Altimeter: Monitoring 43

Chapter 6. When the Fire Goes Out: Hypoglycemia 55

Chapter 7. Burning the Furniture: Sick Days 69

Section Two: The Flashy Plays

Chapter 8. The Supermarket Guerilla: More Nutrition . 87

Chapter 9. Joy to the World: Entertaining 101

Chapter 10. The Road to Zanzibar: Travel 109

Chapter 11. Up Off the Couch! Exercise 119

Chapter 12. The Gown Opens in the Back! And Other
Hazards of Same-Day Surgery 129

Section Three: And Other Things

Chapter 13. Feeling Like a Frog in a Blender? Stress . . . 141

Chapter 14. Caveat Emptor (Let the Buyer Beware):
Patient Advocacy 147

Chapter 15. That'll Be $378.92: Reimbursement and
Coverage for Diabetes Care 159

Chapter 16. Summer Camp: Hormones, Adolescence,
and Diabetes 167

Chapter 17. What Can We Learn from the Black Box?
Research 183

Chapter 18. Is There a History of Death in Your Family?
Complications 191

Index 197

Helpful Tables and Charts

Dynamic Insulin Dosing^{SM} Guidelines 24

Nutrition Basics 40

Monitoring 52

Interpreting Morning Urine Tests for Sugar and Ketones ... 53

Treat Low Blood Sugars with "Newspapers and Logs" 65

When You're Sick 74

Insulin Supplements for Sick Days 75

Foods for Sick Days 76

Sugar-Free Medicines 82

Rules of Thumb for Identifying High-Sugar Foods 92

Picking a Cereal 94

Artificial Sweeteners 95

Alcohol, Insulin, and Type 1 Diabetes 106

Insulin Adjustments for Time Zone Changes 114

Travel Tips for Extensive Trips 115

When You Travel 117

Getting Set to Exercise 126

Stress 145

The Sunshine Laws 155

Resources for Consumers with Diabetes 156

Insurance Benefits Shopping List 164

Section One

The Basics

Chapter One

The Journey
Are You My Doctor?

Not long ago, in a place not far from where you live, a young man named Mike began a journey. On the surface, it seemed to be a simple quest. He was looking for a way to be healthy and live freely in his unique situation.

He seemed to be well equipped to find what he was looking for. He was bright, hard driving, and ambitious. He devoted long hours to the work he loved, and he had the support of good friends and family.

The quest was necessary because, in spite of his many gifts, he had a problem: He had diabetes. And it was getting in the way of nearly everything he wanted and needed to do.

Having diabetes meant getting up early enough every morning for an insulin shot, a blood sugar reading, and a good breakfast. No jumping out of bed at the last minute, skipping breakfast, and sprinting to the train for Mike.

Having diabetes also meant his day was sometimes interrupted by insulin reactions—periods of sweating and confusion brought on by a sudden drop in his blood sugar level. Once he had one while making an important pitch to the top management at work. He had to excuse himself to get something to eat. Now he worries that the boss may see him as weaker or less able than he once did.

And meals were another problem. Business lunches eaten on the run didn't have much in common with the advice the dietitian gave him when his diabetes was diagnosed.

However, lunches were a snap compared to dinner meetings with prolonged "happy hours." Discussing business over drinks could delay a meal for hours. How much could he drink? When should he take his insulin? What's more, the dinners often took place in fine restaurants where the menus offered rich meals and desserts—not the best fare for someone concerned about health.

The list of frustrations seemed endless, but Mike was determined to find a way to take diabetes off the front burner. He was sure his life would get back to normal if only he could keep the diabetes "pot" from always being at a full boil.

His doctor took a different view. He often blamed Mike for the extreme variations in his blood sugar levels. He implied, insinuated, and at times openly accused the young man of "cheating." But sometimes the blood sugar levels were too high even when Mike had followed his diabetes regimen to the letter. The doctor just didn't believe him.

In fact, most of the time, the doctor acted as if Mike's life was getting in the way of his diabetes, rather than the other way around. And so his quest for a better life began with the search for a new doctor.

His first attempt was with a doctor who seemed to solve all of his problems on the very first visit. With a slight smile and a comforting pat on the shoulder, the doctor told Mike to stop worrying so much about his blood sugar.

"That's my job, Mike," he said. "Just take your insulin every day, and I'll take care of everything else."

This seemed like the answer to Mike's prayers. It certainly was easier. What a relief not to continuously worry about his blood sugar. But it wasn't long before he noticed that his energy level was falling and that he was losing weight without trying.

It was a familiar feeling. It was exactly the way he had felt when he first developed diabetes. He was just 16 at the time. He remembered losing weight for several weeks while he grew weaker and weaker. He'd had a terrible thirst that never seemed to go away, no matter how much he drank.

His parents took him to the family doctor in his hometown. The doctor was the one who gave Mike the unwelcome news that he had diabetes. He told him that his blood sugar was near 400. The doctor explained that high blood sugar levels were causing all of Mike's symptoms. He said that when too much sugar gets into the blood, some spills over into the urine, just as water spills over a dam. More and more water is then needed to carry away the extra sugar. Losing all of that water produces the terrible thirst that Mike remembered so well.

The sugar lost in the urine was full of calories—food energy. And that was where the weight loss was coming from. His body used only part of the energy from the food he was eating. The rest flowed out in the sugary urine produced by his high blood sugar level. It was as though he had never eaten that food—and so he lost weight.

One night, when he was thinking about how tired he felt, he noticed an item in a diabetes magazine. It described the Diabetes Control and Complications Trial. The headline of the article said, "DCCT proves that control counts!" The article went on to state that over 1,400 patients with Type 1 diabetes had taken part in the nine-year study. It proved that the long term complications of diabetes could be delayed or even prevented by excellent control of blood sugar levels.

Mike knew that his diabetes was out of control by how awful he felt. And according to the article, he needed to get his blood sugar under control as soon as possible to decrease his chances of developing problems in the future. It was time to resume his journey.

His next stop brought him to a very enthusiastic physician. This doctor agreed that good blood sugar control could help limit the complications of diabetes. Unfortunately, he also viewed normal blood sugar levels as a sort of Holy Grail. He pursued them with a zeal that would have made any Crusader proud.

"Diabetes touches every part of your life, Mike. Everything that affects it has to be carefully managed. Do exactly as I say and I'll have you in control in no time."

Then the doctor took over, putting every detail of Mike's life on a schedule. Even occasional activities such as a game of tennis, were included on the timetable.

It seemed that every hour of the day held some task related to diabetes. Mike began scheduling fewer business appointments. He even canceled meetings entirely on some days in order to get everything done. He was supposed to weigh and measure everything he ate—an impossible task for someone who ate in restaurants nearly every day. But even more frustrating, the doctor's schedule was at odds with the times set for meals and coffee breaks at work. Mike felt his sanity slipping away.

The last straw came when he returned to the doctor's office with his record book. It contained all of the blood sugar values that he had carefully and painfully gathered since his last visit. But the doctor only gave the book a casual glance as he thumbed rapidly through the pages.

Tossing the record book aside, the doctor gazed sternly at the young man. "These blood sugars aren't good enough yet. We need to tighten up your schedule."

Mike's jaw dropped open in disbelief, but the doctor didn't even notice. He was too busy adding more blood sugar readings to the schedule.

"You'll have to get rid of these tennis games, too."

"But isn't exercise good for my diabetes?"

Without even acknowledging Mike's question, the doctor proceeded to further "tighten up the schedule," making even more extreme demands on the young man's time. When he finished, he turned, disappeared through the exam room door, and was gone.

Mike couldn't believe it!

Another appointment had ended and he still didn't have answers to his questions. He had taken a half-day off work and had struggled through traffic to get there on time. And once he had arrived at the doctor's office, he had to cool his heels in a waiting room full of magazines so old that they could have been unearthed in an archaeological dig. But in spite of all that, he had been given less than five minutes of the doctor's time and none of his attention. It was all too much. So was the bill.

It was time to leave...permanently.

So Mike took up the search once again.

Many months, many doctors, and many dollars later, he finally found the doctor he was looking for. The rest of this book is the story of what Mike then learned that put him where he belonged—in control of both his life and his diabetes.

When you control diabetes, it won't control you.

Chapter Two

Riding the Bicycle

An Overview

One evening, the search took Mike to a diabetes meeting at a local hospital. The woman sitting next to him seemed friendly enough, so he began a conversation. As they talked, he realized that even though she had diabetes and understood his problems, she wasn't having the same difficulties herself.

"Your doctors have been taking responsibility for your diabetes," she said. "That doesn't work. What you need is someone to teach *you* how to take control for yourself. Why don't you try my doctor?"

Because the woman seemed to be doing so well, Mike decided to try her doctor and called for an appointment.

A few days later, when he met the doctor for the first time, he blurted out his frustrations. "Doctor," he said, "I want to enjoy my life without thinking about diabetes every minute of the day. I want to work hard, have some fun, and travel. I want to have my old energy level back and to stay healthy. I want to be myself again. Is that too much to ask?"

"No, it's not, Mike. If we work together, I think we can do it."

"I'm glad to hear you say that, Doc. I was beginning to think I was in this all alone."

"No way, Mike. No one manages Type 1 diabetes alone."

"Type 1? You mean some people have a different kind of diabetes than mine?"

"Yes, on both counts, Mike," the doctor replied. "But I think it helps to think of diabetes as something you *don't* have, rather than as something you do. What you *don't* have anymore is a body with the ability to regulate your blood sugar levels automatically. What your body used to do for itself now needs to be done by you, no matter what kind of diabetes you have."

"How many kinds of diabetes are there?" he asked.

"Several," the doctor answered, "But Type 1 and Type 2 are the most common. In the past, Type 1 was called juvenile diabetes and Type 2 diabetes was referred to as adult onset. There is also a type called gestational diabetes."

"What's the difference?"

"In Type 1 diabetes, the cells of the pancreas that make insulin—the beta cells—have been destroyed. We think that their destruction is caused by a problem with the immune system. The immune system's job is to protect us from invading germs. In some people, the system seems to get 'confused' and attacks cells that make insulin as if they were invaders. We don't know why this happens, but the result is that these people lose the ability to make insulin. Without insulin their blood sugar levels increase. Because of this, they have to take insulin shots every day.

"Type 2 diabetes is a different disease." he continued. "Some people with this kind of diabetes make as much insulin as people who don't have diabetes at all. Sometimes they even make more. The problem is that their insulin isn't used effectively, and, therefore, their blood sugar levels rise, too.

"Type 2 diabetes can often be treated with a healthy meal plan, exercise, and pills. All of these treatments help the body's insulin to become more effective."

"Those pills sound a lot better than taking shots," Mike said. "Can I switch to those if I'm really careful about my food and exercise?"

"A good thought, Mike, but I'm afraid it won't work. The diabetes pills aren't insulin. They only help the insulin that's already in the body to work better."

"But why can't they make pills that have insulin in them?"

"If you took insulin by mouth, it would be digested like food and lose its ability to lower the blood sugar."

"How about people with Type 2 diabetes?" he wanted to know. "Do they ever have to take shots?"

"Some do and some don't," the doctor answered. "The first thing that we try is a healthy meal plan and an increase in exercise. If that doesn't bring the blood sugar down to normal, we add one or more of those diabetes pills. If blood sugar levels are still above normal with a good program of food, exercise, and pills, we usually add insulin to the patient's regimen."

"That makes sense, Doc. What was the other kind of diabetes you mentioned?"

"Gestational, Mike. That's a form of diabetes that occurs during pregnancy. In a few women, the blood sugar levels remain above normal after delivery, meaning that they have actually developed Type 1 or Type 2 diabetes. In most women, it goes away after delivery, but it can return later in life, most often as Type 2, but sometimes as Type 1 diabetes."

"How can their diabetes go away?" Mike asked.

"Well, Mike, it's as if the pregnant woman was a small car trying to pull a big trailer up a hill. As long as the load is there, the car has problems. Once the trailer is unhitched, however, that little car can drive along easily, even uphill. In a woman with gestational diabetes, the load created by the growing baby is too great for her capacity to control the blood sugars. But, once the baby is delivered, things usually go back to normal."

"Well, that's really interesting, Doc, but I'm not pregnant, nor likely to be, thank goodness. How can I get my diabetes into control?"

"Do you remember when you were a child just learning to ride a bike? Managing your diabetes is like that. First of all, it takes time. You didn't jump on a two-wheeler and pedal away the first time. In the same way, it will take time to master the skills that will put you in control of your diabetes."

The doctor then pointed out, "Just as no one else could ride the bike for you, no one else can control diabetes for you, either. That's why it's so important that you master the skills for yourself. It's up to you.

"Do you remember the great feeling you had when riding that bike got to be second nature? When you found you could ride it anywhere? So what if a cat ran in front of you or there were potholes in the road? You just made a few corrections and kept rolling right along. Eventually you probably even learned to do tricks on the bike, such as riding with no hands. What a great feeling, even though it gave your mom gray hairs and took years off her life.

"The more you rode, the easier it became. Managing your diabetes will become much easier with practice, too. But first you need to learn the basics."

"What basics?" Mike wanted to know.

"Insulin, food, activity, and timing. Once you understand these, you can play to win. You'll get feedback from blood glucose monitoring. Then you'll use that information to make corrections in either the timing or the amounts of insulin, food, or exercise needed to create even better control of your blood sugar levels.

"When you get that far, you'll be ready to deal with a few potholes in the road such as delayed meals, eating in new places, getting sick, and so on. You'll learn to make the necessary corrections and just keep rolling along."

"You mean I'll be able to do all of that myself?"

"Yes, and, if you want, you can even learn to do the diabetes equivalent of 'trick' riding, such as taking a European vacation or rafting down the Colorado River. We'll talk about that when you've developed a bit more skill.

"But your first job is to learn the basics."

Learning to control your diabetes...

Takes Effort

Takes Time

Takes Practice

But...It's Worth It!

Chapter Three

Keeping the Fire Burning

Insulin

"Regulating your blood sugar is like managing a fire in the fireplace of a cabin in the woods," explained the doctor. "That cabin is like a cell inside your body.

"Blood sugar is the fuel supply for your body's energy-producing fire, just as the logs in a woodpile are fuel for the fire in the cabin's fireplace. Insulin keeps the cabin door open so fuel can be brought in from the woodpile and placed in the fireplace to be burned.

"Without insulin, the door closes, cutting off the fuel supply. When that happens, your body's energy-producing fire can't burn as it should. That's why you must take your insulin every day, without fail. It's as basic to your survival as the food you eat and the air you breathe."

The doctor went on to explain that insulin needs vary from person to person. Each insulin dose must be carefully tailored to fit those needs like a custom-made suit. And insulin needs change a bit from day to day—just as you sometimes need to tighten the belt or loosen the collar button, even when a suit is basically a good fit. The "fit" of the insulin dose has to be adjusted slightly when high or low blood sugar levels tell us it's not quite right.

Mike felt uneasy about the prospect of adjusting his own insulin, and told the doctor so. That was something his other doctors had always done for him.

"Don't worry," the doctor assured him. "We'll be doing this one step at a time. You'll learn exactly how to make small adjustments in your insulin doses using an approach called 'Dynamic Insulin Dosing^{SM}'. Your previous doctors have been using static dosing, which means they set insulin doses at each office visit. Those doses remained the same until your next appointment, even if that next appointment was weeks or even months away."

Mike understood the drawbacks of static dosing firsthand. When his insulin dose was set too high, he had repeated low blood sugar reactions and was eating constantly to "feed" the extra insulin. He felt awful, and his blood sugar levels gradually went out of control.

At other times, when the dose the doctor set was too low, Mike had gone for weeks with high blood sugar levels, waiting for his next appointment and the needed dose change. The high blood sugar levels made him feel tired and fatigued. Once again, his diabetes would be out of control.

The doctor continued, "Because you can check your own blood sugar between office visits using a home blood glucose monitor, we don't have to settle for static dosing and the drawbacks associated with it. We can use Dynamic Insulin Dosing."

"What's Dynamic Insulin Dosing, Doc?"

"It's a simple system you can use to adjust your own insulin doses between office visits. Today I'll estimate your dose based on your current dose, your weight, and the records of your blood sugar levels. But that will only be a starting point.

"Using your blood test results and the Dynamic Insulin Dosing Guidelines, (page 24) you'll make stepwise adjustments in the doses to gradually improve your blood sugar control. You won't waste time waiting around for our next visit. You'll be able to fine-tune the insulin to meet your needs as time goes along. You'll be in charge."

"That makes sense. But it's so different from the way my other doctors have done it," Mike commented.

"It's going to be a big change for you, all right. But Dynamic Dosing will help us get much closer to the blood sugar levels your body maintained on its own before you had diabetes. That's important because keeping your blood sugar levels near normal minimizes your chances of developing the long-term complications associated with diabetes. That's why we want to provide you with every possible tool to improve your diabetes control.

"Dynamic Dosing is a tool. We'll use it as we combine different types of insulin to meet your needs. You see, no one type of insulin can keep your blood sugar in control over an entire day. Sometimes you need a lot of insulin, such as when you eat—and sometimes you only need a little, such as between meals and overnight. You need more than one shot per day and more than one type of insulin to meet the varying demand. We'll use both a short-acting insulin and an intermediate-acting insulin to get the blood sugar control you need.

"Short acting insulins are used to cover food when you eat and to help manage high blood sugar levels when you are sick or out of control for other reasons. There are two types. The one you've been using is Regular insulin. The other is a newer insulin called Humalog, (Eli Lilly and Company, Indianapolis, Indiana). Regular and Humalog look clear, like water. Regular used to be the fastest acting insulin available, but it was much slower than the body's own insulin. That created some problems. Humalog is a great tool because it acts much faster.

"The intermediate-acting insulin we'll be using is NPH. It is a cloudy solution. NPH and Lente, the other intermediate-acting insulins, begin to work more slowly than either Regular or Humalog but their effect lasts much longer.

"By combining mealtime Humalog with NPH in the morning and evening, we can match the ups and downs of your insulin needs as they occur throughout the day and night. It's not the only possible insulin combination, of course, but I think it's the best one for you. That's why we'll try it first. If that doesn't work, we can try other combinations. I have more than one trick up my sleeve!

"I'll write your insulin doses so that the units of Humalog come first. I want you to think of your doses that way too—first the units of clear insulin and then the units of cloudy insulin. That will remind you to always draw-up the fast-acting clear insulin first when you prepare a shot. Drawing up Humalog or Regular insulin first keeps you from accidentally mixing any of the longer-acting cloudy insulin into the short acting. If that happened, your clear bottle of Humalog or Regular insulin would turn cloudy. You'd have to throw it away and buy a new bottle. So remember: first draw up the clear, then the cloudy."

"OK, Doc, I'll remember.

"You were saying that it's important *when* I take my insulin. I guess I've never paid much attention to that. I figured as long as I took it pretty close to meal time—either before or after—it was fine."

"But it's not, Mike. Timing is important. Injecting insulin is like shooting skeet. You have to 'lead' the target. It's as if you were out doing target practice. You would have to shoot ahead of a moving clay pigeon in order to hit it. With insulin, you need to shoot (inject) ahead of the meal—for most people about 30 to 60 minutes before the meal when using human Regular insulin. But those taking Humalog insulin need to inject no more than 15 minutes before the meal. It is much more rapidly absorbed and thus works quicker. Proper timing gets the insulin and food into the bloodstream at the same time.

"The reason we're switching you to Humalog is so that you can take your insulin like you always have—right when you eat—but the result will be much better. You'll get good blood sugar control right after you eat and you won't have as many problems with low blood sugars between meals."

"Why?" Mike asked.

"Because, strange as it sounds," the doctor replied, *"not* properly timing the meal with your insulin actually increased the chances of having a low blood sugar reaction several hours after eating."

The young man found that very hard to believe and said so.

"Let me show you what I mean." The doctor drew two graphs on a small piece of paper. Each graph had two curves on it to represent the effects of Regular insulin and food. The doctor pointed to the first graph and continued. (See Figure 1, on the next page.)

"Not timing the meal properly with your insulin produces 'curve mismatch.' That's what happens when the major action of your insulin occurs at a different time than the major effect of food from your meal. Having a lot of insulin around when just a little food is available increases your risk for having a

Figure I

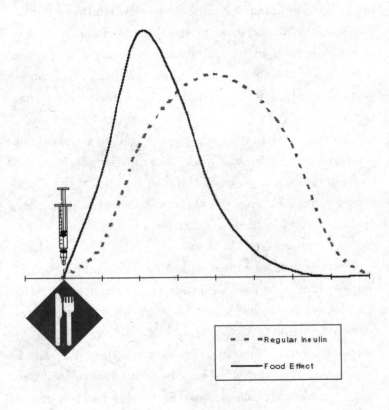

low blood sugar reaction. "Now look at what happens when you lead the target. (See Figure 2 on the next page)

"Notice how the curves match more closely. This produces better blood sugar control. But the truth is that most people find it very difficult and worrisome to take their Regular insulin so long before eating. They forget. Or they may not be sure that they're actually going to be able to eat a half-hour or more in the future. Besides, Regular insulin stays in the blood stream much longer than the blood sugar from most meals. Therefore, it creates a risk for low blood sugars between meals, even when you manage to get the timing right.

"Look at the curves when Regular is compared with Humalog," the doctor said as he drew a third graph. (See Figure 3 on page 23.)

"Humalog begins to work more quickly. It also disappears from the blood much faster than Regular insulin. That means that you might be able to do away with the snacks that you had to be so careful about when you were taking Regular. Between meal snacks are often necessary with Regular to 'feed the insulin,' because Regular stays in the bloodstream long after you have eaten. With Dynamic Dosing, we'll get your background insulin adjusted so that you have less risk of low blood sugars between meals, better control after eating, and more flexibility in both food choices and timing."

"OK, Doc, if you say so, I'll give it a try." And off he went, determined to ride this bike called diabetes.

Figure 2

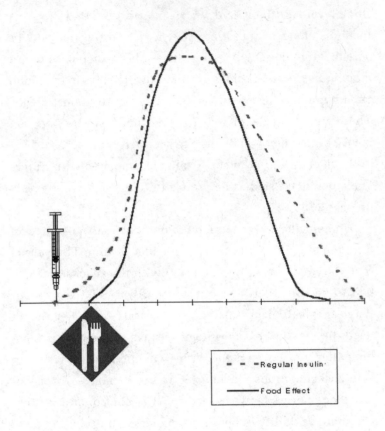

Regular Insulin

Food Effect

Figure 3

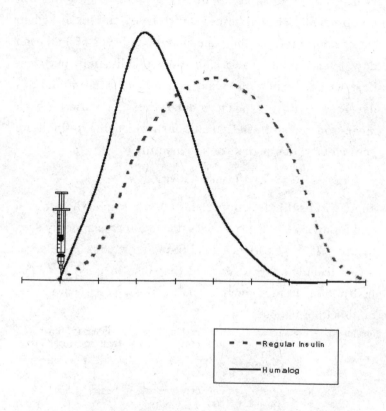

- – – Regular Insulin
- —— Humalog

Dynamic Insulin Dosing Guidelines

Dynamic Insulin Dosing is a method for improving blood sugar control between office visits by making small, timely insulin dose changes based on finger-stick blood sugar tests. It is used when there is no illness present to alter insulin requirements. The guidelines shown below are for use when eating approximately the same amount and type of food each day. If you are eating a variable diet and adjusting your clear (fast-acting) insulin for what you eat, use the guidelines developed with your team to determine your dose for each meal. You can still use Dynamic Insulin Dosing to fine-tune your cloudy intermediate-acting insulin.

Insulin Activity

To adjust insulin, it is important to understand when it acts. The following chart summarizes the action of commonly used insulins. It also suggests a good time to test your blood sugar levels to judge if your dose of that insulin is correct. The instructions in the Dynamic Insulin Dosing charts are based on this information.

Insulin Type	Injected	Has Its Major Effect	Effect Is Shown By Blood Sugar Test
Humalog*	With any meal	In about 60–90 minutes	3–4 hours after shot
Regular	45 minutes before breakfast	Between breakfast and lunch	Before lunch
NPH or Lente	Before breakfast	Between lunch and supper	Before supper
Regular	45 minutes before supper	Between supper and bedtime	At bedtime
NPH or Lente	Before supper or at bedtime	During the night	During the night and before breakfast

*Eli Lilly and Company, Indianapolis, Indiana

High Blood Sugars

The following list of insulin dose changes is based on a blood sugar "action point" of 140. The "action point" is the highest acceptable blood sugar value in each person's desired range of control at a specific time in the day. If your highest acceptable blood sugar level is higher or lower than 140 for the times shown, substitute your own value for 140 in the chart.

If your blood sugar levels **before breakfast** are greater than 140 for three days in a row (and not caused by illness or extra food): Beginning on day 3, increase evening NPH or Lente by 1 unit.

If your blood sugar levels **three to four hours after any meal covered by Humalog** are greater than 140 for three days in a row (and not caused by illness or extra food): Beginning on day 4, increase the Humalog dose for that meal by 1 unit.

If you do not use Humalog, and your blood sugar levels **before lunch** are greater than 140 for three days in a row (and not caused by illness or extra food): Beginning on day 4, increase morning Regular by 1 unit.

If your blood sugar levels **before supper** are greater than 140 for three days in a row (and not caused by illness or extra food): Beginning on day 4, increase morning NPH or Lente by 2 units.

If your blood sugar levels **before bedtime** are greater than 140 for three days in a row (and not caused by illness or extra food): Beginning on day 4, increase supper Humalog or Regular by 1 unit.

Low Blood Sugars

If you have a low blood sugar reaction or blood sugar under 70 **between bedtime and breakfast** (and it was not caused by a delayed meal or increased physical activity): Reduce tonight's NPH or Lente by 2 units.

If you have a low blood sugar reaction or blood sugar under 70 **up to four hours after any meal covered by Humalog** (and it was not caused by a delayed meal or increased physical activity): Reduce tomorrow's dose for that meal by 2 units.

If you have a low blood sugar reaction or blood sugar under 70 **before lunch** (and it was not caused by a delayed meal or increased physical activity): Reduce tomorrow morning's Regular by 2 units.

If you have a low blood sugar reaction or blood sugar under 70 **before supper** (and it was not caused by a delayed meal or increased physical activity): Reduce tomorrow morning's NPH or Lente by 3 units.

If you have a low blood sugar reaction or blood sugar under 70 **between supper and bedtime** (and it was not caused by a delayed meal or increased physical activity): Reduce tomorrow's supper Humalog or Regular by 2 units.

Remember...

- Insulin is needed every day. Missing a single dose can result in serious problems.
- Insulin is best taken at the same time each day.
- Human Regular insulin works best when taken 45 to 60 minutes before a meal.
- Humalog works best when taken no more than 15 minutes before a meal.
- With Dynamic Insulin Dosing and your doctor and educator's help, insulin can produce good blood sugar control.

Chapter Four
Feeding the Flames
Nutrition

A few days later the young man returned to the office for his first visit with a diabetes educator.

"I've never heard of a diabetes educator. What do you do exactly?"

"Well, the title is pretty descriptive," she replied. "It's my job to help you learn what you need to know to take control of your diabetes. Most educators are nurses or dietitians specially trained in both diabetes and teaching. We usually work in the offices of doctors who specialize in diabetes, or for hospitals that have diabetes education programs."

She continued, "There's a lot to learn about diabetes, and learning takes time—more time than most doctors can really give. So educators are usually the ones to teach people with diabetes about their insulin, how foods effect their blood sugar levels, how to care for their feet, and so on. We'll get to all of those things eventually, but we'll take it one step at a time. Do you know where you'd like to start?"

"Eating!" Mike said. "Trying to figure out what to eat drives me crazy. Lately I've just been avoiding sugar and eating pretty much everything else. But I have a hunch that's not enough. Some foods seem to have a bigger effect than others—even foods without sugar, such as pasta and pizza. But isn't there a simpler way to handle my diet than weighing and measuring everything I eat? I've tried that before and I just couldn't keep it up."

"Well, you're right, Mike. What you eat *is* important," the educator said, "and there's a lot to learn. Let's start with something simple: the basics of *what* you eat, *how much* you eat, and *when* you eat it. Later, you may want to learn how to read nutrition labels. Or, you may also want to know what kinds of foods can help cut your risk for heart disease. Eventually, you'll probably want to learn a meal planning system, such as carbohydrate counting or exchanges to help you get even better blood sugar control and more freedom in the foods you choose. But for now, we'll start with the basics: *what* to eat, *how much* to eat, and *when* to eat it.

"What to eat is pretty straightforward," she continued. "You don't really need special foods or elaborate menus. The same foods that were enjoyable and 'good for you' before you had diabetes are still your best choices. All of us feel our best when we eat regular meals that include vegetables, fruits, grains, and low-fat protein and dairy foods. Look at the food guide pyramid on your morning cereal box. It shows how a combination of these food groups make up a healthy diet.

"In fact, rather than calling it a Diet, let's just call it a Healthy Meal Plan. It's the type of meal plan that everyone should consider, and it includes a lot of options. The word 'diet' sounds so rigid. It makes people think that they have to walk around hungry all day or avoid certain foods entirely. That's not the case at all."

"Well, that's good to hear," Mike said. "Once I had a doctor who gave me a sheet of paper with a low-calorie diabetic diet on it. I went to him because my diabetes was out of control and I was losing weight. But on his diet, I lost even more weight and I felt awful. I was always hungry. He gave me a low-calorie diet even though I'd never been overweight in my life."

"That sometimes happens when you get a pre-printed diet sheet. They almost never fit your own needs. Besides, people like different foods; everyone's taste isn't the same. You just can't give everyone the same diet and expect them all to do well. That's why everyone with diabetes really needs to spend time with a dietitian or a diabetes educator who can provide personalized nutrition advice. We'll start today."

Mike replied, "Well, that diet sheet sure didn't work for me. But I do need *some* guidelines because eating right definitely involves a lot more than just avoiding sweets."

"You're so right, Mike. In fact, did you know that many experts no longer recommend that people with diabetes completely avoid sugar and other sweet foods. Simply avoiding sweets won't give you the control you need. Control is the result of balancing what you eat with the proper insulin regimen. Eating lots of sugar can contribute to poor blood sugar control, but so can eating too much of just about anything," the educator explained.

"Of course, you don't have to worry about this if you are willing to go on my Snowflake Diet."

"Snowflake Diet? You're kidding me!"

"No, I'm not. I think it would work but no one has been willing to try it yet."

"What's in it exactly?"

"It's very simple. You can eat all you want of all the foods that don't affect blood sugar levels. Water, both hot and cold, ice, ice cubes, ice chips, ice blocks, ice shavings, and of course, snowflakes.

"What do you think?"

"I think I understand why no one was willing to try it. So what you are telling me is that just about everything I eat can affect my blood sugar level. Right?"

"Exactly, Mike. Instead of putting so much emphasis on merely avoiding sweets, we now advise people with diabetes to eat a healthy diet and keep track of all the starches and sugars they eat. These are called carbohydrates. All foods raise blood sugars to some extent, but carbohydrate foods such as bread and fruit have a greater effect than fats and proteins do. Keeping track of carbohydrates is a simple and effective tool for improving blood sugar control. You can't always tell how much carbohydrate a food contains by looking at it, though" she pointed out. "That's why you should eventually learn to read food labels. That can be a big help in matching the carbohydrate in what you eat with your insulin. But we're going to start more simply than that. I want to see what you're eating now and show you how to control your blood sugar while eating your normal meals. While we're doing this, try to eat a variety of foods at every meal and snack and then write down what you eat," the educator continued. "Combinations that provide carbohydrates with small amounts of protein and fat will produce more stable blood sugar levels."

She handed Mike a piece of paper that read:

Include foods from both groups in meals and snacks

Larger portions of carbohydrate foods	Smaller portions of low-fat protein foods
Bread	Meat, lean
Cereal	Milk*, low-fat or skim
Potatoes	Fish
Rice	Chicken
Beans*	Low-fat cheese
Crackers	Beans*
Noodles	Tofu
Fruit	Natural peanut butter

For best health, portions of carbohydrate foods should be larger than portions of protein foods. Try to keep carbohydrate portions about the same size from day to day.

*Milk and beans contain both carbohydrate and protein

"I understand," said Mike, "but *how much* of these foods should I eat?".

"There are two things involved in answering that question," she said.

"The first is the total amount of food you need and the second is the amount you eat at any one time.

"First, let's talk about the total amount of food you need each day. The amount of energy, or calories, you need depends on a number of things. They include your size, your level of physical activity, and whether you're a man or a woman. What you need isn't affected by the fact that you have diabetes or how much insulin you're taking. Simply put, you need enough food every day to provide the energy your body will use. In Type 1 diabetes—the kind you have—you can't achieve good blood sugar control by eating less than your body needs."

This was news to Mike. He'd often tried to eat less when his blood sugar levels were high. Sometimes he would even skip a snack because of high test readings. It seemed so logical, even though he had to admit it hadn't worked very well.

The educator continued, "With Type 1 diabetes you need as much food every day as it takes to provide the energy your body will use. Starving yourself isn't a good way to get your blood sugar levels under control. Blood sugar control comes from matching your insulin to the amount of food you actually eat every day. Your appetite is a very good guide to the total amount you need to eat.

"Now let's talk about how much you should eat at one time," the educator continued. "Think again about building a fire in the fireplace of your cabin. If you were depending on that fire to keep you warm all through a cold winter's night, you wouldn't throw all of the wood on the fire at once."

"Why not?" he asked.

"Because, if you did that, the fire would blaze madly for awhile, and quickly burn up all of the logs. The fire would probably be out before morning. But if you took the same amount of wood and fed it to the fire slowly throughout the night, in the morning you'd still have a nice warm fire. You might even have some logs left over."

She explained further, "Eating to help control your diabetes is like feeding logs to that fire a few at a time. Dividing up your food throughout the day will keep the fire burning evenly. You'll have a warm, well controlled fire all through the day and night, instead of a raging inferno that later goes out because of a lack of fuel. Your hunger will be controlled and you'll have a good level of energy throughout the day."

This sounded good to Mike. She then went on to explain the relationship between Mike's insulin and his meals.

"Your insulin program of Humalog before meals and NPH in the morning and evening looks like this."

She drew a small picture to show Mike when his insulins act. (See Figure 4 on the next page.)

Figure 4

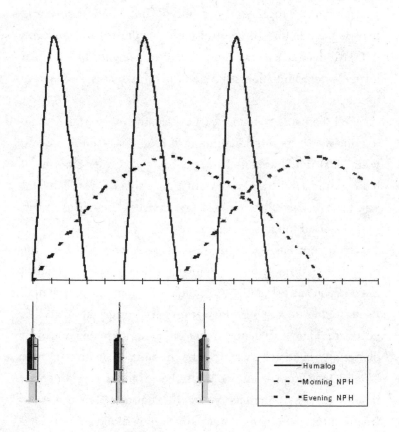

Humalog

Morning NPH

Evening NPH

"Humalog acts faster than the Regular insulin you used to take and doesn't stay around as long. So we can use the Humalog to target the individual meals and use the NPH to provide the proper amount of background insulin that your body needs.

"Using this approach, you might not need the snacks between meals that you would with Regular insulin. But you will still need a bedtime snack. We will use your blood sugar levels to determine the best plan of insulin, meals, and snacks for you.

"We'll be using Dynamic Insulin Dosing to get your Humalog doses adjusted to the amount of food you usually eat and your NPH doses adjusted to provide the proper amount of background insulin. If you want to eat snacks, you can. But you probably won't have to snack to 'feed' the extra insulin that you used to have between meals.

"Once your basic insulin doses are set, you will have the option of learning to adjust your insulin to the actual amount of food you eat. After all, some days you're more hungry than usual. Other days, you may not be very hungry at all. When you didn't have diabetes, your pancreas adjusted for your changing appetite by varying the amount of insulin in your blood. Once you get some of these basics taken care of, you'll be able to 'play pancreas' yourself. That can give you more freedom than you've had ever since your diabetes was diagnosed."

"That reminds me of something I don't understand," Mike said. "Why is my blood sugar lower on an afternoon when I have a steak and salad for lunch rather than my usual sandwich and milk? I know the steak has more calories."

The educator complimented Mike on being so observant and then explained, "The starches and sugars in the bread and milk in your usual lunch are all converted to blood sugar—100 percent. The steak doesn't contain any carbohydrate, only protein and fat, and the salad has very little carbohydrate. About half of the calories from the protein and less than 15 percent of the fat end up as blood sugar. So even though the steak has more calories, it has less impact on the blood sugar level. You had a reaction because your insulin was adjusted for your usual lunch that contained more carbohydrate than the steak and salad.

"Until you learn to adjust your insulin for changes in food intake," she went on, "you will need to eat similar servings of bread, cereal, pasta, milk, fruit, and other carbohydrate foods at the same meal each day. Having twice as much fruit at breakfast or half as much bread at lunch will make a big difference in your blood sugar levels. That's because the change in carbohydrate intake alters the balance between your food and a set dose of insulin."

"So what I eat really does make a difference. Does it matter when I eat, too?" Mike asked.

"Yes, it really does. That old saying 'Timing is everything' is certainly true of diabetes," the educator answered.

Mike mentioned the doctor's advice that he take his Humalog right with his meal—no more than 15 minutes before eating. "I learned the hard way not to take my insulin and then fiddle around in the kitchen for an hour getting my meal together. I did that the first week I was on Humalog and I started to get low before I'd even decided what to eat. Thank goodness I was surrounded by food. But what if my blood sugar level is high before I eat? In the old days when I had a high blood sugar level before a meal, I used to take my insulin and then wait for it to begin lowering my blood sugar before I ate."

"I'm glad you asked, Mike, because that's not an approach we recommend. We want you to maintain that close timing between your meals and insulin at all times. Waiting for your insulin to lower your blood sugar and then eating later will only give you a high blood sugar level later in the day. Remember, Humalog acts quickly and disappears quickly. If you take it too long before eating, there won't be any around to control your blood sugar when you do eat. That amounts to throwing a big log on the fire at the wrong time," she said. "It can cause a great increase in blood sugar levels later in the day because of 'curve mismatch.' The delayed meal creates a big demand for insulin after the insulin's strongest action is past. For now, we just want you to follow the Dynamic Insulin Dosing Guidelines when these things happen."

"I like to eat less when my blood sugar levels are high," said Mike. "Like a couple of weeks ago. My blood sugar was 236 at bedtime, so I skipped my bedtime snack. I don't think it's a good idea to push a high blood sugar level even higher by eating."

"I know that sounds logical, Mike. But remember the story about feeding logs to the fire gradually to keep it going all night. When you skipped your bedtime snack, you increased your chances for having a reaction in the middle of the night."

Mike wrinkled his forehead. "Do you mean having a high blood sugar level at bedtime doesn't protect me from having a reaction overnight?"

"Don't count on it. Remember that your overall goal is to match food peaks and insulin peaks. A blood sugar peak at bedtime doesn't match up with the peak of insulin that acts overnight. That peak comes hours later. After all, 12 to 15 hours can go by between your evening meal and breakfast.

You've been taking your evening NPH before supper. That means that the insulin's major action is between about midnight and 4 a.m. That's a very high-risk time for low blood sugar levels. That makes your bedtime snack important—even when your blood sugar level is higher than you want it to be at bedtime."

Mike was shaking his head. "Gee, when I came in here today I thought the most important thing about my diet was avoiding sweets. It's definitely more complicated than that. Not only do I have to think about my food choices, but I also have to pay attention to how much I eat and when I eat it."

"Definitely," she said. "But the more you learn, the more foods you'll be able to enjoy without disturbing your diabetes control. For now, concentrate on choosing a healthy variety of foods and eating about the same amount at the same time each day. We'll write down some menus based on your usual meals to help you with that. Later on, when the rest of your basic education about diabetes is complete, we'll move on to some more involved issues."

Nutrition Basics

- Good diabetes control begins with a varied and healthful meal plan.

- Eat enough food to maintain your ideal weight. If you're losing weight without dieting, check your diabetes control.

- Until you learn more advanced techniques, eat about the same amount of food at the same time each day. Delaying or skipping meals and changing the amount of food you eat can destroy the balance between food and insulin.

- Keep learning about food and diabetes. The more you know, the more choices you have.

- A personalized meal plan prepared just for you by a registered dietitian who specializes in diabetes can make living with diabetes much easier.

Chapter Five

Installing the Altimeter
Monitoring

After Mike had mastered the basics of insulin and food, he and the educator concentrated on how to monitor his diabetes. She told him they would be checking three different measures of diabetes control; two of them would be his responsibility.

"Let's start with blood sugar tests. I know you've been doing finger-stick blood sugars for quite a while, Mike. Now let's talk about how you can use them to really make a difference in your blood sugar control."

"I'll bet you've got another story," the young man observed.

"How'd you guess?" she replied. "Controlling your diabetes is not only like riding a bike. In some ways, it's also like flying an airplane. A pilot flying at 5,000 feet checks his altimeter to find out whether he's at the right distance from the ground. And he doesn't just check it once. He checks it repeatedly, because a single reading could be misleading."

"What do you mean?"

"If he glanced at his altimeter only once and it read 5,000 feet, he could assume he's flying straight and level at the desired altitude. But that single reading could also mean he was passing through 5,000 feet on his way up into the stratosphere. Worse yet, he could be diving through 5,000 feet, toward a close encounter of the painful kind with the ground.

"A good pilot takes a series of altimeter readings to make sure that he's flying straight and level. Blood sugar readings work the same way. A single reading—whether it's low, normal, or high—doesn't tell you all that you need to know. To find out whether you're flying straight and level within your desired range of blood sugar levels, you have to take readings in sequence. Then you can see patterns."

"So, what would you like me to do?"

"I recommend that you test four times each day—before meals and at bedtime."

"That's a lot!" Mike replied.

"I know, but it's the only way to determine where your blood sugar levels are throughout the day. Most of the time, you'll get the information you need from testing before meals and at bedtime. But sometimes, such as when we're trying to pin down how to balance your insulin doses with the amount of food you eat, testing after meals will be helpful. And sometimes testing in the middle of the night is a good idea."

"But it hurts!"

"There are some things you can try to reduce the discomfort. For one thing, it can make a difference exactly where you do the finger stick. Where are you sticking yourself?"

"Here on the tips where there is some padding."

"You might try sticking more towards the sides of your fingers. The very ends, the tips, are the most sensitive. That's because there are so many nerve endings there. There are fewer nerve endings on the sides of the finger pads. But, when you do it on the side of the finger, don't do it next to the nail. That's a very sensitive area, too.

"Also, check out the various finger stick devices that are available. Some of them allow you to adjust just how far the needle goes into the skin. That could help decrease the pain.

"Let me give you some samples of the newer lancets that are thinner. They are another option for decreasing your discomfort.

"Currently, researchers are working to develop blood glucose monitors that do not need a drop of blood to work. If those become available, you would not even have to prick your finger to get a blood sugar result."

"Well, Kate, that's really great for the future. Unfortunately, the future's not here yet and I've really gotten burned out on doing these finger sticks. Lately, I've only been testing in the morning and when I feel high or low."

"I won't pretend that what I'm asking is easy, Mike. But you'll get a much better picture of your overall control by testing four times in one day than you would by testing four times on four different days. The reason for this is that your blood sugar levels change during the day. Just because you have a normal reading in the morning doesn't mean that your readings will be normal during the rest of the day, too. You've told me you want to keep your blood sugar levels near normal so you can feel your best and reduce your risk of complications. If that's still your goal, let's try initially to keep the readings between 80 and 180 most of the time. Once your level of control stabilizes in that range, we'll know we've worked out a rough match. After that we will be able to pick your own blood sugar target range and fine tune things to achieve it."

"It'll be great to have my diabetes in control once and for all," said Mike.

The educator shook her head. "I have to be honest with

you, Mike. That's not going to happen. Getting your diabetes under control is more like a journey than a destination. You're always on the road. Your life and your diabetes are a little different each day. That means that blood testing, watching your food and Dynamic Dosing have to go on all the time to keep your blood sugar levels near normal."

"I wish I didn't have diabetes."

"That's an understandable and common reaction. It's no fun. A lot of my patients have told me the same thing, Mike. I'll tell you what I've told some of them. 'You don't have to have diabetes any more, if you don't want to.'"

"I don't?"

"No, Mike. When you check out today at the front desk, just tell Trish that you've had enough and that you don't want diabetes any more."

"Really? What will she do then?"

"She'll go looking for someone to trade with you. I'll bet there are plenty of people out there who would be willing to trade your problems for theirs."

"So you're pulling my leg after all," Mike said. "I'll just stick with the disease I already know, but it never lets up, does it?"

"No, it doesn't. But even though *diabetes* never lets up, *you* may need to lighten up occasionally! Testing four times a day is what's needed to keep your blood sugar levels in control. It's what the doctor and I recommend: the ideal. But I'll also tell you that I've never had a patient who stuck to that ideal 100 percent of the time. If you feel like the demands of taking care of your diabetes are really weighing you down, it may be better to relax and lighten up a bit: test less frequently for a while or do less record keeping. When you do those things, your blood sugar control will probably slip. But that may be an acceptable price to pay in the short term to protect your motivation to keep at it over the long haul.

"If you do cut back on testing occasionally, I suggest that you still test four times a day at least one day a week. This will help make sure things don't get too badly out of control while you're taking your break. Remember, four tests in one day always tell us more about your control than four tests on four different days."

"So less testing means less control," Mike observed, "but testing four times a day will keep my blood sugar levels in line?"

"It's a big help," she agreed, "but don't expect your blood sugars to always be in the target range, even when you've done everything 'by the book.' Occasional unexplained high blood sugar levels are part of having diabetes. They can occur because of many other things that we haven't even talked about; things such as the other body hormones that can raise blood sugar levels. However, since you don't have any control over them, we haven't really talked about them yet. The point is this: Perfect blood sugar readings are not your goal. That's just not possible. Instead, try to get the majority of your blood sugar readings in the target range most of the time. That's why we use blood sugar patterns to adjust your insulin, instead of responding to a single high blood sugar reading.

"Because of advances in our ability to care for diabetes, we are now able to do a much better job than we did in the past. But we still don't have the technology to keep all of the blood sugars in the normal range all of the time. Scientists and medical doctors are working on this, and perhaps one day they'll come up with tools that will make perfect control possible. Until that happens, we need to set goals that are actually realistic.

"Also, Mike, remember that there's no such thing as a 'bad'

blood sugar reading. Your blood sugar record only contains pieces of information. Whether a reading is above, below, or within your target range, it's still useful information you can act on to maintain or improve your diabetes control."

Mike hesitated, then said, "That sounds good in theory, but I think I'll still feel disappointed when my blood sugar levels are way off the mark."

"That's only natural. But disappointment is different than guilt. Feeling like there's something wrong with you just because your blood sugar is out of range doesn't help matters. I'd much rather see you focus on doing something with the numbers than on beating yourself up about the fact that they're where you want them to be.

"Now let's talk about the second sort of test that we'd like you to do regularly: urine testing."

"Urine tests?" asked the young man. "I thought those were obsolete now that we do finger-stick blood sugars. I know for a fact that urine sugar tests aren't very accurate."

"You're absolutely right. Urine tests for sugar really aren't very accurate as a way of knowing what your blood sugar levels are," the educator agreed. "But we recommend you test your urine, not just for sugar, but also for ketones." (See "Interpreting Morning Urine Tests for Sugar and Ketones" on page 53 for help understanding the results of this test.)

"What's a ketone?"

"Ketones are chemicals that show up in the urine when your diabetes is getting out of control. Blood sugar testing doesn't tell you whether you're producing ketones or not because blood glucose meters can't measure them.

"That's why we recommend urine ketone testing for everyone who has Type 1 diabetes. We also suggest that people with Type 2 diabetes who take insulin do this test when they're sick. Later, I'll give you guidelines for how to use urine ketone test results. For now, all I want you to realize is that urine testing for sugar and ketones is part of our overall plan for keeping track of your diabetes."

"OK, I can wait. But you said there was a third kind of test I should know about."

"It's called a glycosylated hemoglobin test. Years ago, the only tool a doctor had to judge how well someone's diabetes was being controlled was a fasting blood sugar test. The doctor did one of these every few weeks or months. They had serious drawbacks."

"Really?"

"Yes. Their main weakness was how little information they gave the doctor. It was almost impossible to recommend helpful changes in the insulin dose or meal plan based on a single fasting blood sugar reading. And just as important, they couldn't give the doctor a clear picture of how well the management plan was working. There wasn't any way to know what the 'average' blood sugar had been since the last visit.

"And, for the person with diabetes, going into the doctor's office to have blood drawn for a fasting blood sugar was far from ideal. The best that he or she could expect was a hungry morning spent waiting for the blood draw. Sometimes the doctor was delayed, making it even more difficult. Most of the time, the patient's routine was badly upset because he waited to take his insulin until after he'd seen the doctor. Of course, that would throw off the timing of meals and insulin for the whole day. The blood sugar levels would almost certainly go out of control. We've talked before about how critical timing is to controlling your diabetes."

"I know," Mike said. "I've been in that situation more than once."

"These days, finger-stick blood sugar tests give us a lot more information. And it's information that's especially helpful in managing day-to-day changes in food, insulin, and activity.

"But each finger-stick blood sugar, just like a fasting blood sugar, only measures one point in time. Before you developed diabetes, your body was constantly monitoring your blood sugar levels so your pancreas could add the proper amounts of insulin to your bloodstream 24 hours per day. I know that doing four finger-sticks a day seems like a lot. But it still only tells us what's happening at four split seconds during the day.

"You know how much blood sugar levels can vary. Because of this, even though they're so helpful, your blood tests still may not reveal a true picture of your overall blood sugar control."

"So what do we do?"

"Well, that's where the glycosylated hemoglobin test comes in. It allows us to see what your blood sugar control has been like over the past several weeks."

"I know hemoglobin has something to do with the blood," Mike said, "but what in the world is glycosylated?"

"Picture one of your red blood cells as an apple," the educator answered. "If we dipped the apple in sugar syrup, it would come out coated with a certain amount of sugar. The thicker the syrup, the thicker the coating of sugar on our candied apple.

"Red blood cells have a life span of about 120 days. As they move around the body in the bloodstream, they pick up more or less 'sugar coating,' depending on the amount of sugar in the blood. That sugar coating process is called glycosylation. It's going on every minute of every day.

"By periodically taking a blood sample and sending it to

the lab, we can, in a sense, check the amount of sugar coating on the candied apple. If there had been a lot of sugar in the bloodstream during the last few weeks, the glycosylated hemoglobin will be above normal. If the average blood sugar levels had been in the target range, the glycosylated hemoglobin will be lower. Our goal is a reading as close to the normal range as possible."

"You mean the same reading as for a person who doesn't have diabetes?"

"Yes, or close to it."

"Are there any other tests that I'll need to have done to help me monitor my diabetes?"

"There are other tests that we will follow, but they are not used to monitor your diabetes. Their job is to help us check for any effects diabetes might be having on your overall health."

"What are they?"

"Once or twice a year, the doctor will do a urine microalbumin test. This will help him determine whether the diabetes has affected the kidneys. If it has, he will begin administering medication to protect the kidneys and help them work better."

"What kind of medication will he use?"

"They are called ACE inhibitors."

"It sounds like a card game," Mike replied. "Does the doctor also have King or Queen inhibitors? If he does, I could sure use them when I play poker with my friends!"

They both laughed.

"Are there other tests I'll need?" Mike asked.

"You need to see the eye doctor at least once a year to check your eyes for any changes due to diabetes."

"Eye problems have always been a big worry to me. If there are changes, can anything be done?"

"Yes, Mike. Getting checked every year guarantees that any changes that happen will be found at an early stage. Early changes in the eyes, called retinopathy, can usually be treated with laser if they are found early enough."

"Well, sign me up for those yearly tests then," Mike said. "There sure is a lot to keep track of."

"Yes, and that's not everything," Kate replied. "Periodically the doctor will also order tests on your cholesterol. We'll also be following your blood pressure at every visit. He will also check your feet regularly."

"Wow, and I thought having diabetes meant that you only had to test blood sugars."

Mike left the office thinking what a change it was to be working with people who listened. He was pleasantly surprised to have his questions answered in ways he could understand.

Monitoring

- Finger-stick blood sugar tests show your pattern of blood sugar control.
- Patterns tell you far more than any single blood sugar value.
- Testing urine for sugar and ketones can provide additional helpful information.
- Glycosylated hemoglobin helps reveal overall diabetes control.
- Tests of the eyes, feet, cholesterol, and kidney function should be conducted regularly to check for developing problems.

Interpreting Morning Urine Tests for Sugar and Ketones

The following chart explains the results of urine tests for sugar and ketones. It is based on testing the first urine passed in the morning. The guidelines are true for people who begin to show sugar in the urine when their blood sugar gets higher than 180. This is true for most people, but exceptions do occur.

Negative Sugar/Negative Ketones Overnight blood sugar stayed between about 70 and 180. This is the goal.

Negative Sugar/Positive Ketones Overnight blood sugar did not go over 180. Ketones indicate a low blood sugar reaction may have occurred.

Positive Sugar/Negative Ketones Overnight blood sugar went above 180.

Positive Sugar/Positive Ketones Overnight blood sugar went above 180, and the ketones indicate your diabetes is out of control.

Chapter Six

When the Fire Goes Out

Hypoglycemia

Time passed. Mike's blood sugar levels were improving. They were lower than they'd ever been since he developed diabetes—so much lower, in fact, that he was now frequently having low blood sugar reactions. He was frustrated. If good control meant having reactions so often, then he didn't want any part of it.

"I'm really sick of insulin reactions!" he complained to the doctor. "I feel so rotten when my blood sugar bottoms out that I'm tempted to keep it on the high side. Most of them are happening at night, which scares me. I never had this many reactions when my blood sugar levels were high. Now that I'm in tight control, I feel worse than ever."

"But you're not in tight control, Mike," the doctor explained. "Having frequent reactions means your diabetes is out of control—out of control on the low side. When we began working together, your diabetes was out of control on the high side. Your reactions are telling us that we overshot the mark. But there is a solution. You need the next installment in the saga of the log cabin to understand how low blood sugar levels happen, and how to prevent them."

He reminded Mike that insulin holds the cabin door open so wood can be brought in to feed the fire. Then he asked what would happen if the supply of wood ran out.

"Well, the fire would go out," he replied.

"And that's exactly what happens when there isn't enough food around when your insulin is acting. The body's energy-producing fire goes out. The body recognizes this situation as a real threat. It tries to correct the problem by releasing certain chemicals called hormones that raise the blood sugar: glucagon, epinephrine, growth hormone, and others. Besides raising your blood sugar, they can cause some pretty uncomfortable symptoms.

"What kind of symptoms do you have when your blood sugar levels become low?" the doctor asked.

"I usually get shaky and break out in a sweat," the young man answered. "And at night, I sometimes have nightmares. There have also been times when I've gotten confused and was kind of bumbling around."

The doctor explained to Mike that it's important for each person to know and watch out for his or her own particular symptoms of falling blood sugar levels.

"Symptoms can range from weakness and shakiness to headaches or tingling around the mouth and lips. In fact, low blood sugar levels can cause almost any symptom that your body can have. For instance, stomachaches, dizziness, and feeling nervous can all be caused by low blood sugar levels. That's why it's a good idea to check your sugar anytime you're not feeling right. That's the only way to know positively whether you're having a reaction."

The doctor continued, "The symptoms can get severe. When you lose your coordination or get confused, it's a sign the brain isn't getting enough fuel. You might even pass out if a reaction that severe goes untreated."

"That's scary," Mike said.

"You're right about that. And the scariest part is how a reaction that severe could lead to a serious accident if it happened while you were driving your car or climbing a ladder or doing something similar. Besides, repeated severe reactions can cause brain damage. At the very least, reactions make you feel awful. And in the worst case, they put you in real danger."

"What can I do about it?"

"Quite a bit," the doctor replied. "There are things I can do and things you can do. We'll try them all. Most reactions can be prevented by applying the knowledge you already have about how food, insulin, and activity affect your blood sugar levels.

"Remember when we first met, I compared managing your diabetes to riding a two-wheel bike? Well, if you keep everything centered when you're riding the bike, you keep your balance and pedal along without any problems. But if you lean too far one way or the other, the bike falls over.

"It's the same with diabetes. Think of skipping a meal, going for an unplanned run, or changing the time you take your insulin as leaning too far over on the bike. All of these can produce curve mismatch—a situation where your need for insulin doesn't match the amount that's in your blood—setting you up for a low blood sugar reaction.

"So, what *you* can do is to make sure that you're paying attention to all of these factors. What *I* can do is to move your evening NPH insulin from suppertime to bedtime.

"This will help to even out the spread of insulin so that at any one time you will have less insulin on board. This should then help to decrease your chance of having a low blood sugar reaction.

"But it means taking another shot each day."

"Doc, one more shot is no big deal if it will cut down on these miserable reactions.

"But what should I do if I do have one," the young man asked. "I usually feel terrible when it happens. And it seems to take so long before I begin to feel better. I generally end up stuffing myself before I feel human again."

"In an insulin reaction, the fire is going out. You need to get it going again as quickly as you can. So use something that burns fast and hot. It's like using newspapers or small twigs to start the fire in the cabin's fireplace. High sugar foods that are quickly digested act as 'newspaper.' Glucose gel or tablets, fruit juice, and regular soda pop are best because they act quickest. Some of my patients even carry small tubes of cake icing. Hard candy and fruit will also do the job.

"Quick-acting sugars will help you feel better faster than other foods, but they only support the blood sugar for a short time—sort of like newspapers that help start the fire but won't keep it going for very long. So, if the next meal is more than an hour away, you'll need to put a 'log' on the fire."

"What's a log?" Mike asked.

"Logs are foods such as peanut butter sandwiches, meat sandwiches, or cheese and crackers. They contain carbohydrate, protein, and fat. They release sugar into the bloodstream more slowly than fruit juice and other high-sugar foods. This helps prevent you from having another insulin reaction before the next meal rolls around."

"I usually just move up the time of my next meal. That gives me logs, right?"

"It gives you logs all right," the doctor agreed, "but it's not the best way to handle a reaction. Changing the time of your meal and insulin can increase your risk of having another reaction later on."

"What do you mean?"

"Remember when you were on human Regular insulin and would eat supper at about 6 p.m.? Well, let's say that you had an insulin reaction at 4:30 p.m. and decided to eat supper and take your insulin right away."

"I've done that."

"So far so good, but the problem comes a little later in the evening. On a normal day, the food from your 6 p.m. supper would have matched up with the Regular insulin you injected at about 5:15 p.m. But that day you ate your supper at 4:30 p.m. because of the reaction. By the time your evening insulin begins to peak, your supper is digested and long gone. You're probably going to run out of fuel and have another reaction later that evening."

"I've done that, too! So, even with the Humalog, I'll do better if I eat my meals at the usual times, and treat lows with 'newspaper and logs?'"

"Right," the doctor agreed. "By the way, keep in mind you won't always feel symptoms when your blood sugar is getting too low."

"I learned that the hard way," Mike said. "Last spring I had a reaction that came on without warning. I literally didn't know what hit me until I woke up to find myself looking into the eyes of a big, sweaty paramedic."

"I'll bet that was excitement you could have done without," the doctor said.

"That's called an asymptomatic reaction, meaning you did-n't have any symptoms. It happens if your body doesn't release the hormones we talked about when your blood sugar begins to fall. Asymptomatic reactions are more common in people whose blood sugar levels have been in poor control for many years. This can be a permanent change and can be very risky. But you know from your own experience, they can happen to other people, too.

"Because you can't always rely on getting symptoms when your blood sugar is too low, my advice is to treat any blood sugar of 70 or less with 'newspapers and logs.'"

"Why do you pick 70?"

"Because home blood glucose meters are only accurate to within 10 to 15 percent of the actual blood sugar value. They'll get you 'in the Ball Park' but won't necessarily give you the exact value. For example, if we sent your blood sample to the lab and got back the exact blood sugar value of 100, your meter could show any value between 85 and 115 and still be working just fine."

"But, Doc, that's quite a spread."

"That's the best you can do with these machines."

"You've got to be kidding. That doesn't sound very good."

"It's good enough to keep you in control of your blood sugar. There is another choice, though. If you like, you could spend $35,000 on the type of machine the lab uses and carry it around with you in a moving van."

"Very cute, but I think I'll stick with my meter."

"Wise choice. Meters are great, Mike, but they're not perfect," the doctor went on. "We just need to use what we know about how precise they are. For example, in the case of a finger-stick blood sugar reading of 70, the true blood sugar could actually be lower, as low as the high 50s. So rather than risk a crash, I recommend you treat any blood sugar of 70 or lower immediately—even if you feel just fine."

"Immediately?" Mike asked. "Even if I'm doing something important, such as trying to make it to a business appointment on time?"

"Yes. Begin treatment immediately, at the first sign of a reaction. The longer you wait, the worse the reaction can get and the harder it can be to treat. Also, keep in mind that it's sometimes possible to feel as though you are having a low blood sugar reaction even though your blood sugar is above 70. This can happen if blood sugar levels drop quickly. The body senses this and its alarm system goes off even though the actual blood sugar has not yet fallen below 70. So if you're having symptoms of a low blood sugar reaction but your blood test comes out between 70 and 100, go ahead and treat it with 'newspaper.' If you feel better after treating it, then you know that was the reason why you were feeling bad. If there isn't a change in how you feel, that wasn't the problem."

"So, Doc, let me see if I have this straight. If my blood sugar is below 70, I should treat it immediately, whether I feel symptoms or not. When my blood sugar is between 70 and 100, I should only treat it if I have symptoms; but if I'm feeling good, I should leave it alone."

"That's right, Mike."

"And Doc, what about headaches? I'm confused. You said that low blood sugar reactions can cause almost any symptom that my body can have. So I guess it can cause headaches, too?"

"Yes it can."

"Well, if that's the case, how can I tell if a headache is caused by a low blood sugar or by the stress of my job? Sometimes when I'm working hard preparing some of my reports and have deadlines to meet, I get headaches. Should I just take an aspirin?"

"No, what you need to do is find out whether the headache is due to your blood sugar being too low or due to some other cause."

"How can I do that?"

"Easy, Mike. Just take your glucose meter and do a finger stick. It will let you know whether your blood sugar is too low. If it is, go ahead and treat it. If your sugar is not too low, then go ahead and treat your headache with a pain relief medicine, such as acetaminophen or aspirin.

"Remember, if it is a low blood sugar reaction that you are treating, begin treatment right away, even if it means getting to an appointment late. I think it's better to arrive a little late than to arrive somewhere confused or not at all because of a serious low blood sugar reaction."

"You mean like the one I had when I passed out. Could I have done anything to save that visit from the paramedic?"

"Yes, that was definitely a severe reaction. In that case, glucagon could have helped."

"Glucagon?" Mike asked. "What's that?"

"It's a hormone that works opposite to insulin. A shot of insulin moves sugar out of the bloodstream and into the cells, causing the blood sugar to fall. A shot of glucagon moves sugar out of the liver and into the bloodstream, causing the blood sugar level to rise.

"When you can't eat, glucagon is the best way to treat a severe low blood sugar reaction."

"What do you mean 'when I can't eat'?"

"Well, for example, if you were sick to your stomach and were throwing up, you would not be able to keep any food down. If you then had a low blood sugar reaction, you would not be able to treat it, unless you had glucagon."

"Gee, I never thought about that," Mike replied.

"If you had glucagon, you could give yourself a shot and solve the problem.

"Another example would be if you passed out because of a low blood sugar reaction. You would not be able to swallow anything. If someone put food in your mouth, you could choke. But if they gave you a glucagon shot, that would save the day.

"And remember, even though your blood sugar will go up after a glucagon shot, don't expect it to happen right away. After it's injected, it may be 10 to 15 minutes before the blood sugar level begins to rise and you wake up. Once you're awake, the glucagon should be followed by 'newspaper and logs'.

"But if you can't take the 'newspaper and logs' because of throwing up, give me a call."

"What would you do?"

"If we couldn't stop the vomiting with medications, I'd hook you up to an IV that had sugar water in it. That would stop your blood sugar from going any lower."

"Why couldn't I just keep using glucagon?"

"Because glucagon can't be used very often. You see, Mike, the liver is like a warehouse full of sugar. Glucagon opens the doors of the warehouse and lets the sugar out. Once that sugar is gone, there isn't any left to replace it. If you went into another reaction fairly soon, giving another shot of glucagon might not help because the warehouse would be empty. We need to refill it—replace the stored sugar that the glucagon released. Once you stop throwing up, you can refill it by eating. But while you're still throwing up, we have to refill it by giving you sugar through an IV in your arm."

"I guess the bottom line is to keep my meals, insulin, and exercise in balance to prevent reactions, but prepare for any reactions that might still come along."

"That's right, Mike."

The doctor then gave Mike a prescription for a Glucagon Emergency Kit™. "Get a couple now, before you need them. Keep your glucagon in an easy-to-find place at home and at work. Your friends, family, and close co-workers should learn how to use it. They're the ones you'll be relying on to use it if you should ever have another severe reaction. It needs to be mixed just before it's used. It's injected just like insulin."

"But, Doc, how could I have planned in advance for this problem? Once I took my morning dose of insulin at night by mistake, rather than my evening dose. My morning dose is much larger than my evening dose."

"Mike, that happens more often than you might think. Because you can't get the insulin out of you once it's in there, you need to eat extra food to balance it. If that ever happens again, check your blood sugar and eat a snack at least every three hours during the night."

"In other words, I need to eat my way through it."

"That's right. And, Mike, one last reminder. Don't forget to wear your diabetes identification at all times. It could save your life if you're ever found unconscious. While it's best to keep the bike balanced, it's still a smart idea to wear a helmet, just in case."

Treat Low Blood Sugar Levels with "Newspaper and Logs"

1. Identify the Reaction

- Be aware that any symptom might be caused by low blood sugar levels.
- Know your own usual symptoms of a low blood sugar reaction.
- Do a finger-stick blood sugar test if you're not sure.

2. Begin Treatment Immediately

- If your blood sugar is 70 or less, begin treatment immediately, whether you're having symptoms or not.
- If your blood sugar is between 70 and 100, treat only if you're having symptoms.
- Delay allows the reaction to become more severe and difficult to treat.
- Delay can result in unconsciousness.

3. Start the Fire with "Newspaper"

- Eat two or three glucose tablets or one package of glucose gel.

OR

- Drink eight ounces (or more) of fruit juice or regular soda pop.
- If none of the above is available, eat anything sweet.
- Eat the next meal on time. Don't eat it early because of the reaction.

4. Keep the Fire Going with "Logs"

- If the next meal or snack is less than an hour away, no "logs" are needed.
- If the next meal or snack is more than an hour away, treat as above, then add a "log" to the fire.

- Logs are foods that provide carbohydrate, protein, and fat, such as a meat, cheese or peanut butter sandwich, or a glass of milk.

5. Prepare in Advance for Severe Reactions Resulting in Loss of Consciousness

- Obtain a Glucagon Emergency Kit
- Instruct family and friends in its use.
- If you pass out, they should inject glucagon immediately.

6. Always Wear Your Diabetes Identification

Chapter Seven

Burning the Furniture

Sick Days

The next few weeks passed peacefully. Mike was finally beginning to feel he had control over his diabetes, instead of the other way around. He had a few low blood sugar reactions, but they were mild and he was prepared to treat them. He was absorbed in his daily activities at home and at work. And his blood sugar levels were right where he wanted them to be. Most were in the target range that he and the doctor had agreed on. Life was going well. He had his old pep back. As he walked into the diabetes educator's office, he almost shouted out the good news.

"This is the best part of my job, Mike. It's great to see what a change you've made using the information we've talked about. I'm delighted you're so satisfied with the results, too.

"But our work's not over," she continued. "Now that you've learned to ride the bike on the straight and narrow, it's time to get ready for obstacles. You need a plan for riding the bike when the weather turns bad—when you get sick."

"But I'm fine," he protested. "Why do I need to think about getting sick now? I just want to enjoy this big improvement."

"I understand that," she replied. "But once you're sick, it's too late to do everything possible to make the situation better. By being prepared, you can keep a garden-variety illness such as the flu or a cold from destroying the control you've worked so hard to achieve."

"OK, you win. I'm ready for another story. Am I going to ride the bike, go flying, or return to the log cabin?"

"The log cabin. How about if I go with you this time and keep you company?" she offered. "Let's pretend we're in the log cabin on a freezing winter's night. We're relaxing in front of the fire, talking about something other than diabetes."

"Well, at least we took a break."

"Yes, but the fire is dying down, and we've used up all the firewood you brought in earlier. You head for the door to bring in more wood from outside, but there's been a fierce storm and ice and snow are blocking the door. It won't budge."

"Things are going from bad to worse here! What else can go wrong?"

"You try the windows, but they're frozen shut, too. The cabin's getting cold. The fireplace flames are sputtering."

"Sounds like a real crisis," Mike said. "What do we do?"

"We've got to keep warm. We'll freeze if we let the fire go out. So there's only one thing left to do."

"What's that?" Mike asked.

"We'll have to burn the furniture to keep warm. And so we start to pitch it into the fireplace. Obviously, this isn't a perfect solution. The furniture has paint, varnish, and stain on it. It's a different kind of wood than the firewood. It gives off choking black smoke as it's burning. The wood from the woodpile gave off clean white smoke. But at least we'll stay warm until morning."

"Saved by cheap chairs and our own ingenuity!" he said.

"You're really getting into this, Mike. But don't forget there's a point to the story. Think of the storm as an illness—a cold, the flu, or other infection. More strength is needed to hold a door open when a stormy wind is blowing. In the same way, during an illness, the cells of the body have more difficulty holding open their cell doors so sugar can enter and be burned for energy.

"Without the fuel provided by sugar, the cell needs to find another way to keep its energy-producing fire going. So it 'burns the furniture.' In this case, the furniture is the fat inside the cell. When fat is burned for energy without sugar being available to burn with it, ketones are produced. They're just as noticeable as the black smoke from the burning furniture in the cabin."

"I've been sick a few times since I've had diabetes," said Mike, "but I've never seen any 'black smoke.'"

"That's because you weren't testing for ketones in the past. Now we have you test when you're sick so you'll notice as soon as possible if you're 'burning the furniture.' If that happens, we need to bring it to a halt as soon as we can."

"Why do we need to stop it?" the young man wondered. "Most people probably have plenty of 'furniture' to burn."

"It's important because, just as the black smoke from burning the furniture in the cabin polluted the air, large amounts of ketones can be dangerous as well. They will eventually make the whole body too acidic. The combination of too much sugar building up in the bloodstream with ketones and excess acid is a life-threatening condition called diabetic ketoacidosis. We call it 'DKA' for short."

"I don't like the sound of 'life threatening,' even if it does have a nickname. What should I do if I find I'm burning the furniture?"

"Here's a list of several things to do when you're sick," the educator answered. "Let's begin with your insulin."

"I know I have to take my insulin every day without fail, but shouldn't I reduce the dose when I'm sick and not able to eat as much as usual?" the young man asked.

"No, but that's a common mistake," she answered.

"Remember that when you're sick, the storm is raging, making it harder for the doors to the cells to remain open. That's why you need to take at least your usual amount of insulin. In fact, you may need to take extra insulin on top of your usual dose just to keep those doors open. If the doors don't open, sugar will begin to rise in the bloodstream because it can't get into the cells.

"Also, when you're sick, a number of hormones released by the body can raise blood sugar levels even more."

"But how can that happen if I don't eat?" asked Mike.

"Besides being a warehouse where sugar is stored, the liver is also a factory. It can actually make new sugar under certain conditions. The factory makes and releases sugar at a much higher rate when we're sick than when we're well. It doesn't need food to do that. So even if you haven't eaten a thing, you might find your blood sugar getting higher because of the liver."

"How do you stop the liver from doing that?"

"You use insulin. Insulin will slow down the sugar-producing factory in the liver and help bring things under control," she explained.

"I get it. Not taking your insulin when you're sick can make matters worse by allowing the liver to make all that extra sugar."

"Exactly. That's another reason why it's vital to always take at least your normal dose of insulin and never skip a dose, even when you're sick and can't eat. When the storm is raging, you could need extra insulin to keep the sugars under control and correct the ketones. In fact, the doctor might have you supplement your usual dose with extra clear insulin (Regular or Humalog) when you're sick. (See "Insulin Supplements for Sick Days," page 75.) But the most important thing to remember is to stay in close contact with the doctor's office whenever you're sick."

When You're Sick

1. Take at least your usual dose of insulin. Cutting back or skipping a dose of insulin can cause significant problems when you're sick. Add supplements of clear insulin (Regular or Humalog) as indicated.

2. Use "Foods for Sick Days" (page 76) if you're unable to eat your usual meals.

3. Test a double-voided* urine sample for ketones four times a day at the times of your usual finger-stick blood sugar readings.

4. Report vomiting episodes to your doctor immediately.
- Take medicine to control vomiting or diarrhea as directed.
- Drink extra fluids (small frequent sips).
- Use broth or fruit drinks to replace the fluids and minerals lost during vomiting and diarrhea.

5. Maintain contact with your doctor.

6. Know when, and under what conditions your doctor wants you to call.

7. Know how to reach your doctor, especially during non-office hours.

8. If your illness continues or worsens and you can't reach your doctor, go to an emergency room.

---

*See page 79 for a description of how to obtain a double-voided urine sample.

Insulin Supplements for Sick Days

When you're sick, your need for insulin may increase. If this happens, your blood sugar levels will begin to rise. To correct this problem, add supplements of clear insulin (Regular or Humalog) to your usual doses until your blood sugar levels return to normal. The size of the supplement is based on your blood sugar level. If you have ketones in your urine, double the supplement shown for your blood sugar level. Take supplements before meals, but not at bedtime. Extra insulin taken at bedtime could cause a low blood sugar reaction while you're asleep and unable to treat it.

Record all supplemental doses in your log book. Begin taking supplements as soon as you recognize that illness has disrupted your diabetes control. Do not take supplements at other times without consulting your doctor.

For a blood sugar of ...	Add to normal insulin dose:
Less than 200	0 units of Regular or Humalog
200 to 249	1 unit of Regular or Humalog
250 to 299	2 units of Regular or Humalog
300 to 349	3 units of Regular or Humalog
350 to 399	4 units of Regular or Humalog
400 or more	5 units of Regular or Humalog

Double the supplement if ketones are in the urine

Note: Unless advised otherwise by your doctor, only use supplemental insulin when you're sick. When you're well, make insulin adjustments using the Dynamic Insulin Dosing Guidelines.

Foods for Sick Days

When you're not feeling well enough to eat as you usually do, it's still very important to intake adequate amounts of food and liquid. Don't cut back on your dose of insulin or skip any injections. This could lead to major problems.

Even if your stomach is upset or your appetite is poor, be sure to ingest enough carbohydrate (starch and sugar) to cover your insulin. Try substituting one of the following for each serving of starch, milk, or fruit you normally eat:

1/2 cup apple, orange, grapefruit, or pineapple juice

1/3 cup cranberry juice cocktail, grape juice, or prune juice

3/4 cup regular (not sugar-free) soda pop

2 teaspoons of honey

2 1/2 teaspoons of sugar

1/3 cup regular (not sugar-free) Jell-O®

6 LifeSavers®

7 jelly beans

1/2 twin Popsicle®

1 slice bread or toast

6 saltine crackers

1/2 cup hot cereal

1/2 cup ice cream

1/2 cup sherbet

1 cup soup

1/3 cup tapioca or pudding

1/2 cup eggnog

1 cup plain yogurt

In a nutshell, many of the foods you generally avoid when you're well are the ones that can help you when you're sick!

"What about food?" Mike asked.

"Well, you know from experience that you may not feel like eating much when you're sick. Even the types of foods you want, and can tolerate, may change."

"So what should I do? I'm taking my insulin and I have to eat something, right?"

"True. Actually, when you're sick you can eat a lot of things that you probably are pretty careful about when you're well. Here's a list of sick-day foods you should keep handy." (See "Foods for Sick Days," page 76.)

"Hey, this is a list of all the things they used to tell me not to eat because I have diabetes!"

"You noticed that! Actually, the fact that these foods have a large amount of sugar in a small amount of food is what makes them good choices when you're sick. When you don't feel like eating very much, you can probably get enough calories from eating small amounts of them to keep you going and balance your insulin."

"There's sure a lot to know about being sick."

"That's true," the educator agreed. "But it's worth the effort. Doing these things lessens the effect a simple illness can have on your diabetes. And you may save yourself a stay in the hospital."

She then continued through the "When You're Sick" list and discussed the importance of drinking plenty of fluids during an illness. "It's easy to get dehydrated—lose too much water—when you're sick, and it's even easier when you have diabetes. You may not drink as much as usual because your stomach is upset. You may lose extra fluids because you're throwing up or because you have diarrhea. And if your blood sugar level becomes too high, you'll lose even more water through the urine."

"But what if I'm really sick to my stomach and not able to keep much down?"

"Try swallowing small sips slowly. Take your time. It may take as long as half an hour to get down a half cup of fluid when you're sick. Doing it this way may help to 'sneak it' past an upset stomach. If you try to swallow a full glass all at once, you'll increase the chances of tossing it back up."

"What should I do if I can't sneak it past my stomach?" asked Mike.

"I'll have the doctor write you a prescription for a medicine to control nausea and vomiting."

"I'm glad to hear that," Mike said. "There's nothing I hate more than driving that 'porcelain bus' when I'm vomiting!"

"Well, it's certainly not any fun, Mike," Kate answered. "The medicines can save you from that."

"What kind of medicine stops vomiting?" he asked.

"You could use either Compazine tablets, Tigan suppositories, or a Transderm Scopalamine patch. They all require prescriptions, so we will ask the doctor which one he recommends.

"Fill the prescription today so you have the medicine on hand the next time you need it. If you're that sick, you won't feel like running out to the pharmacy to pick up supplies."

"That makes sense. Is there anything else I should keep around the house for the next time I get sick?"

"Yes, remember to keep your Glucagon Emergency Kit handy. As we discussed earlier, if you have a low blood sugar reaction and can't keep anything down because of an upset stomach, you can use your Glucagon Emergency Kit to treat a reaction. Then give us a call.

"Also, keep the doctor's and the pharmacy's phone numbers handy. Get a thermometer so you can tell the doctor your temperature. Get some of the items from the 'Foods for Sick Days' list. Also get a supply of nonprescription medicines that you can use when you're under the weather, such as cough medicine and pain relievers. Some over-the-counter medicines have a good deal of sugar in them, so I'll give you a list of medicines that are sugar-free. They can make it easier for you to stay in control when you're sick." (See Sugar-Free medicines, on page 82.)

"How about testing?" Mike inquired. "Should I test any differently when I'm sick?"

"Blood sugar testing is pretty similar to your normal plan. But because things can change so quickly when you're sick, testing becomes even more important than when you're well. Do at least four blood sugar tests each day, and test any time you think you might be having a low blood sugar reaction but aren't sure."

"How about urine testing? Is that any different?"

"Yes, it is. When you're sick, we recommend that you do a urine test four times a day, at about the same times that you do your finger-stick blood sugars. In this way, you'll know immediately if you begin to 'burn the furniture.' If that happens, call the doctor so he can help you stay on top of the situation.

"I'd like you to use a double-voided urine sample for the ketone tests you do when you're sick. Then you'll be able to tell if you're still making ketones at the time that you do the test."

"What do you mean by a 'double-voided' urine sample?"

"These are terms we use for urine testing. A single-voided sample contains urine made by the body since the last urination, whenever that might have been. For example, the first urine you pass in the morning is a single-voided sample. If you last urinated before going to bed the night before, the morning urine would consist of urine made all during the night. In order to test a double-voided sample, you would empty your bladder but not test the first sample—the single-voided sample. About a half hour later you would urinate again. This is the sample that you would test. This is called the double-voided sample."

"When would I use each one?"

"The single-voided urine sample in the morning is helpful when you're well. It lets you know what happened during the night. (See "Interpreting Morning Urine Tests for Sugar and Ketones," page 53.). It also alerts you to the presence of any ketones. It's like an early warning system that lets you know if you're having problems. The double-voided urine is helpful when you're sick. Because the urine in a double-voided sample was made during the previous half-hour, it tells you how you're doing right at that time. For example, if you test a single-voided urine and find ketones, you don't have any way of knowing exactly when they were made. If it's been six hours since you last urinated, the ketones in the urine sample could have been made at any time during that six-hour period.

"If the ketones were made only during the first hour, it would mean that you're improving. You might need less insulin than if you were still making ketones. A double-voided urine lets you see how you're doing right now. If there are ketones in it, you know that you'll need extra insulin to treat them."

"There's more to this than I ever realized," Mike said. "I can see a lot of things are going to be different the next time I get sick."

Mike left the educator and headed for home. On the way, he stopped at the pharmacy to pick up his sick-day supplies.

Then he went to the supermarket and stocked up on Jell-O, soda pop, and Popsicles. As he stood in the candy aisle picking out a bag of jelly beans to keep around for sick days, he thought to himself with a smile, "If my other docs could only see me now!"

Sugar-Free Medicines

Some medicines (such as painkillers, cough medicines, and antacids) contain sugar. The amounts are generally small and may not disturb your diabetes control. But since illness makes it more difficult to control your diabetes, it's best to choose sugar-free varieties when you can.

If a doctor prescribes a drug for you that contains sugar, ask if there is a sugar-free alternative. Read labels before you buy over-the-counter. Avoid those that contain sugar (sucrose, glucose, sorbitol, mannitol, fructose, or dextrose) or alcohol. Read the label every time you buy a product. Manufacturers occasionally change their formulations.

Decongestants

Afrin® Nasal Spray

Dimetane® Decongestant Elixir

Neosynephrine® Nose Drops

Rynatan® Tablets

Sinutab® Maximum Strength Nighttime Liquid

Cough Medicines (sugar-free, containing little or no alcohol)

Cerose® DM Liquid

Colrex® Cough Syrup

Contac® Jr. Liquid

Hytuss® Tablets

Tolused-DM® Liquid

Pain and Fever Medications

Acetaminophen (generic name)

Datril®

Dolanex® Elixir

Ibuprofen (generic name)

Panadol®

Children's Panadol® (liquid, drops, tablets)

Sick Day Summary

1. Always take your insulin, even if you can't eat.

2. Keep a supply of sick-day medications on hand.

3. Use 'Foods for Sick Days' when you're too sick to eat your usual meals.

4. Drink plenty of liquids.

5. Take your temperature and record it daily while you're sick.

6. Keep the doctor's and pharmacy's phone numbers handy at all times.

7. Check and record blood sugar and urine ketones at least four times a day while you're sick.

8. Call the doctor if ketones are present.

The Flashy Plays

Chapter Eight

The Supermarket Guerilla

More Nutrition

Mike paced up and down outside the double doors. He was waiting for the diabetes educator in front of the biggest supermarket in town. When he'd asked her last week how to pick out a cereal that wouldn't send his blood sugar sky high, she'd said it was time for a "tour." It seemed a little silly. After all, he'd been in supermarkets all his life. He hoped he wouldn't see anyone he knew.

He felt a tap on his shoulder. "Am I late, Mike?"

"No. Actually, I was a little early. Gee, Kate, couldn't we do this in the office? I feel a little strange about walking around the supermarket reading food labels."

"If you're really uncomfortable, we can skip it. But if you look around while we're in there, I think you'll see a lot of people reading labels. And not all of them have diabetes. Everyone who's trying to watch their weight, cut their risk for heart disease, or just eat a healthy diet needs to know exactly what they're buying. We could do this lesson in the office, but we couldn't do as good a job. Besides, I think seeing and handling the foods will help you remember what we talk about. What do you think?"

"OK, I guess I can take it," Mike replied. "Lead on, general. Where do we start?"

"Funny you should call me 'general,' Mike. One way to think about shopping these days is sort of like a military campaign. There are thousands of possible choices in every supermarket. Tonight's tour is like boot camp. I'm going to make you into a 'supermarket guerrilla.' You'll be learning to use weapons that will help you defend your blood sugar and your arteries against some other great military leaders: General Mills, General Foods, and Cap'n Crunch! Let's hit the battlefield."

As Mike and Kate walked into the store, he pulled a grocery cart out of the line-up.

"As long as we're here, I might as well pick up a few things," he explained. "You know, when I first started seeing you, you said to cut down on foods with too much fat and sugar. So I tried reading labels a few times, but I got discouraged. Everything's made with sugar. I can't even find any bread that I like that doesn't have sugar or honey or some other sugary thing in it."

"Amazing, isn't it?" she commented. "But you've brought up an important point: it's probably not possible to avoid sugar. But that's OK, because it's not really necessary to totally avoid it."

Mike picked out a head of lettuce and some tomatoes and put a 10-pound bag of potatoes in the bottom of the cart. "Well, I finally figured out that much. When I finally gave up and bought the whole-wheat bread with molasses in it, nothing drastic happened to my blood sugar. But how do I know where to draw the line? Some sugary things such as regular soda pop shoot my blood sugar way up. How much sugar is too much?"

"Well, you're going to hate the answer to that one, Mike. It depends. Sugar that you eat doesn't necessarily have to get in the way of blood sugar control. Remember, we talked earlier about controlling all the carbohydrates in your diet in order to do that. And sugar—like all carbohydrates—does need to be counted if you have diabetes. That's where reading labels comes in. Let's head on over to the bread aisle where I can show you exactly what I mean."

While they walked, Kate continued, "Some people want to limit refined sugars in their diet as an overall health measure. And in my little dietitian's heart, I feel that's a great idea. Sugary foods don't usually provide a lot of nutritional payback in vitamins and minerals. Nevertheless, by using the nutrition label, if you want to, you can learn how to eat foods with refined sugars occasionally without losing control of your blood sugar.

"You may not know it, but you've already been using one of the supermarket survival weapons I talked about earlier: the ingredient list. We're going to upgrade your use of the ingredient list from the novice to the expert class right now. Do they have the kind of bread you've been buying?"

"Here it is," he replied, "Orowheat 100% Whole Wheat Light. See, here's the molasses on the ingredients list."

"Exactly how far down on the list is it?" she asked.

"It's the seventh item down on the list. Does that make a difference?"

"Yes. That's helpful information if you're trying to keep the total amount of sugar in your diet on the low side. The list is arranged in decreasing order. The ingredient contained in largest amount is listed first. The ingredient contained in the second largest amount is listed next, and so on, until we get to the ingredient that there is the least of. It's listed last.

Seeing where sugar appears on the list gives you a general idea of how much is in the food. A good rule of thumb for people trying to limit refined sugars is to look for foods that don't have sugar, or other sugary ingredients, in the first four ingredients. Molasses is seventh on your bread label. Sucrose, dextrose, honey, brown sugar, corn syrup, corn sweeteners, and fruit juice concentrate are other high sugar ingredients to watch for."

"So my bread is a keeper for the basket," Mike said as he tossed in two loaves of bread.

"That's true, Mike," Kate answered. " We know that it's a good nutritional choice; the first ingredient is whole wheat and there's not much refined sugar in it. Keep in mind that even healthy foods can raise your blood sugar levels. Before we're done today, we'll talk about how to use The Nutrition Facts label to keep everything in balance. But, first, let's finish talking about sugar. What are you going to remember from what we've talked about so far?"

"That I shouldn't buy foods that have any of those sugar words in the first four ingredients?" he asked.

"Well, you should at least stop and think before you buy them. When a food you want has sugar in the first four ingredients, your decision about whether to buy it or not depends on a couple of things. First, think about how much you'll be eating at one time. If it's something that you just use a dab of, such as ketchup or sweet pickle relish, it's probably OK. Second, find out if there's another brand of the same item that doesn't contain sugar. Look at these two peanut butter labels. What do you see?"

"Sugar's second on the list in this one," said Mike. "The other one only has peanuts and salt in it. Look. The one without sugar has oil floating on the top. The other one doesn't.

Which one should I take?"

"The one with the oil is the better choice, Mike," said Kate. "That oil is on top because it's natural peanut butter that has not been processed. Processed peanut butter is high in saturated fat and that is why the oil has not separated and floated to the top. Saturated fat raises cholesterol and is bad for the heart."

"Hey, I like the natural peanut butter better anyway. Another keeper."

"Here's something else, Mike. Tell me what you can about these granola bars."

Mike squinted to read the small print on the label. "Well, corn syrup is third on the list and molasses is fourth. It's even got brown sugar farther down the list. Pretty sweet, huh?"

"Right. Foods that have several sugar ingredients aren't a great choice for everyday use. But here's another 'it depends.' They might be perfect to carry on a long bike ride where you're using up lots of blood sugar exercising. When you learn to adjust your insulin for changes in food intake, you'll also have the option to 'play pancreas' and take the extra insulin needed to cover the granola bar if you want to. Once you've gotten to be a great label reader and you feel you're ready, we'll figure out a ratio of insulin to carbohydrate. You can use it to help you figure out an appropriate insulin dose for every meal you eat, no matter how large or small it may be.

"There's room for just about any food in a healthy meal plan. To make it work, you just need to figure out how much of the food to use and when. Even regular soda pop has its place. When you're sick, it can help you sneak calories into a queasy stomach, and when you have a low blood sugar, it's easy to find soda just about anywhere."

Rules of Thumb for Identifying High-Sugar Foods

1. Know all the "sugar words":
- sugar
- molasses
- honey
- dextrose
- corn syrup
- corn syrup solids
- high fructose corn syrup
- fruit juice concentrate

2. For better overall nutrition, avoid or limit foods in which a "sugar word" appears in the first four ingredients.

3. If a "sugar word" is in the first four ingredients, ask yourself:
- How much will I use at a time? If the amount is very small, such as ketchup for example, it's probably OK.
- Is there another brand of the same thing made without sugar? For example, peanut butter or fruit spreads.
- If you're going to eat it anyway, read the Nutrition Facts label to learn how much carbohydrate is in each serving. Use that information to either
  - Fit the food into your meal plan, or
  - Adjust your meal-related insulin to cover what you eat.

4. If there are several sugary ingredients, question the food's use. You may want to limit the portion or limit that food's use to high energy demand situations such as heavy exercise.

"Well, I'm not getting much exercise right now, but I'll keep the granola bars in mind if I get to go skiing this winter. However, what I am doing is eating breakfast every day. How do I pick a cereal that doesn't send my blood sugar off the scale?"

"That's what got us down here in the first place, isn't it? Well, this brings us to the supermarket guerrilla's other major weapon: the Nutrition Facts label. These labels show the serving size for the food and the amounts of certain nutrients that you get from a serving that size. As a tool for blood sugar management, the Nutrition Facts label has only two items that you need to be concerned about: the serving size, and the Total Carbohydrate. Always be sure to check the serving size. Sometimes a surprisingly small serving size is shown to make the nutrition information look more acceptable. Here's the cereal section. We couldn't have missed it. I think it's bigger every time I come to the store. Notice that the serving size shown for some dense cereals such as this granola is only one-quarter of a cup. When you eat a whole bowl full of this, you get about four times as much carbohydrate and calories as for the same volume of a cereal such as Cheerios that has a one-cup serving size."

"I thought that keeping the size of my cereal serving the same every morning would be the best way to standardize my breakfast. That's obviously not enough," he said.

"It's not enough unless all the cereals you eat have about the same amount of carbohydrate in a similar size serving. Let's check out the cereals you normally buy."

"Most of the time I eat Cheerios, but I also keep Shredded Wheat and Honey Nut Cheerios around. Let's see, the Cheerios have a one-cup serving size with 15 grams of carbohydrate and they are low in sugar. I knew those were a keeper because my blood sugar's generally fine after I eat them. Hey, here's one of my problems. Honey Nut Cheerios have 15 grams of carbohydrate in a half-cup. Well, now I know why my blood sugar goes through the roof when I eat these. I get twice as much carbohydrate and sugar in the same size bowl of the Honey Nut as I do from the regular Cheerios."

"Well, obviously your morning insulin is well-adjusted to the amount of carbohydrate in a bowl of Cheerios. Until you begin to adjust your own doses, you need to stick with about that same amount of carbohydrate at breakfast. Would you be happy eating half as much of the Honey Nut kind to get that amount of carbohydrate?"

"No way. I want a full bowl of cereal. I guess I'll have to find something else. I used to like Kix when I was a kid. Is that one OK?"

Kate handed Mike a box of Kix. "What do you think, Captain? I just gave you a field promotion because you're doing so well."

Picking a Cereal

1. **Cereals that have 5 grams or less of "sucrose and other sugars" are "low sugar."** They are a good choice for people trying to limit the total amount of refined sugar they eat.

2. **To simplify eating a variety of cereals on different days, pick cereals that have about the same serving size and the same amount of carbohydrate per serving.** Then eat the same size serving each day.

3. **If you want more variety, control serving size to get the right amount of carbohydrate for you.** For example, if your insulin is adjusted to cover 1 1/2 cups of Cheerios (23 grams of carbohydrate), you could only eat 1/4 cup of Grape-Nuts(to get the same amount of carbohydrate (unless you learn to adjust your insulin for changing meal size).

4. **Whole grain cereals are good nutritional choices because of the extra fiber and nutrients they provide.**

"The Kix look good. They're low in sugar and the serving size and amount of carbohydrate per serving is about the same as the Cheerios. That will give me some variety without sending my blood sugar too high or limiting me to a tiny portion. Oh, that reminds me, what about things that are made with artificial sweeteners? Are they OK for me to eat?"

"Well, sure, Mike. Remember, even regular soda pop has its place but the question is when and how much. Foods that are artificially sweetened fall into two general categories. Things that have very few calories, such as Sugar-Free Jell-O, artificially sweetened drink mixes, and diet pop, fall into one group. You can use them in reasonable amounts without a lot of thought. They won't affect your blood sugar much at all.

Artificial Sweeteners

1. Find a non-caloric tabletop sweetener you like for use in beverages and on cereal. If you like to bake, find one that's stable in cooking.

2. Read the Nutrition Facts labels of all artificially sweetened foods. They may have calories and carbohydrates from other ingredients that do affect blood sugar levels. Remember, total carbohydrate is what's important to blood sugar control.

3. Artificially sweetened foods that have very few calories, such as diet soda, sugar-free gelatins, and low-calorie jellies, can be used freely.

"But there's another group of artificially sweetened things that is entirely different," Kate said. "I'm talking about things such as sugar-free pies, cookies, candy, pudding, and hot cocoa mix. These foods contain ingredients that have carbohydrates and calories that need to be taken into account. Take, for example, this sugar-free pie. Some people assume they can eat as much as they want without raising their blood sugar because the label says 'Sugar Free.' But a small piece contains 245 calories and 40 grams of carbohydrate. It's not exactly like diet soda!"

"You can say that again. This sugar-free pudding has 12 grams of carbohydrate, the same as a glass of milk," Mike said. "I think I'll get some to put in my lunches. Sometimes I can have a pudding instead of a carton of milk with my lunch and just drink a diet soda. Thinking about lunch reminds me, what's the story on low-fat lunch meat? Is that what I should be eating?"

"In some cases, those lower fat lunch meats can be a pretty good choice, Mike. But when it comes to advertising, remember, 'The large print giveth and the small print taketh away.' Even when the big words on the package look promising, you still need to read the Nutrition Facts label to know exactly what you're getting.

"Cutting back on saturated fats—the kind you get in meats, dairy products, hydrogenated fats, and lard—is one of your most powerful weapons for keeping your blood cholesterol level down. A lower fat lunch meat such as turkey salami has less animal fat than traditional salami, but it's still not what would be considered a low-fat meat. If you've just got to have salami occasionally, picking the lower fat one makes sense. But there are other sandwich fillers that are lower in fat and usually less expensive. For example, sliced turkey breast and boiled ham are both naturally low in fat."

"Are you kidding?" Mike asked. "I thought ham was really high in fat."

"No, ham's actually made from a low-fat pork cut. And it's especially lean when the surface fat has been trimmed away in processing. Look at this Danola Danish Ham. It's got 35 calories and 1 gram of fat per slice and only 26 percent of its calories come from fat. If you put that on some great crusty rye bread with dark mustard, you've got a very low-fat lunch."

"You know, Kate, that one piece of information made this whole trip worthwhile. Into the basket with the boiled ham. Are there other fats that are a better choice than the saturated kind that you mentioned earlier?"

"Yes, Mike. The monounsaturated and polyunsaturated fats found in most vegetable oils are better at keeping your heart healthy than the saturated fats found in meat and dairy products. Monounsaturates are found in canola oil, olive oil, avocados, and nuts. Those are some of the best choices as far as fats are concerned, although the total amount of fat in your diet should be kept fairly low. Corn oil, safflower oil, and sunflower oil are all good sources of polyunsaturated fats. Use them in cooking and in salad dressing and find a margarine that lists the liquid form of one of them as its first ingredient.

"Saturated fats are another matter. Because they play such a big role in raising your blood cholesterol level, I've suggested before that you switch from whole milk to skim or one percent and pick lean cuts of meat. But there are other sources of saturated fat that you need to read labels to avoid. Look out for palm oil, coconut oil, and anything that says 'hydrogenated.' Although those ingredients might be called 'vegetable' on the label, they're just as hard on your heart as pure lard. They're cheap and they have a long 'shelf life.' Unfortunately, they might shorten *your* shelf life, so try to avoid them. They show up in a lot of processed foods such as crackers, cookies, frostings, and snack foods."

"So I'm helping out my heart when I pick these wheat crackers that have liquid safflower oil in the ingredients instead of these cheese flavored ones that say 'partially hydro-genated cottonseed oil."

"That's right, Mike. Your basket's getting pretty full."

"You noticed. There's not much room left, actually. Looks like I'm going to eat well this week. One thing I've been wondering about, though. We haven't spent any time in the dietetic food section. Shouldn't I be shopping down there?"

"Well, there may be a few things down there that would be useful to you, Mike. A lot of the people I work with keep sugar-free pancake syrup around and one or two kinds of sugar-free jelly on hand. However, don't be fooled by the words 'dietetic' or 'diabetic.' The biggest mistake people make shopping in the diet section is to think that all the foods there are good choices. They're not. You have to be just as careful about reading the labels of dietetic foods as you are of other foods.

"For some items, there may be a better tasting, cheaper version of the same thing in the regular food section that isn't much different nutritionally. Out here in the rest of the super-market, there are fat-free crackers, low-fat mayonnaises, and salad dressings made with good oil instead of coconut oil. 'Diabetic' cookies, for example, are often sweetened with sorbitol or fructose. While those sugars don't raise blood sugar as quickly as table sugar, they have just as many calories and not everyone likes their flavor. Regular cookies, either ones you make at home or buy in the supermarket, can be part of your meals. Just make sure you know how much carbohydrate they contain. Then use that information to keep your food and insulin in balance.

"Look at these simple cookies, for example. Gingersnaps and vanilla wafers are fairly low in calories and carbohy-drates. They could be a great choice."

"Do most of your shopping where the 'real' foods are, Mike. There's a whole world of good food out there that's good for you: fresh fruits and vegetables; chicken, fish, and lean meat; low-fat and skim-milk dairy products; potatoes, rice, pasta, bread, and cereal. When you eat convenience items such as cold cereal, lunch meats, crackers, cookies, snack foods, and bread, read the labels. Know what you're eating. Then you can make good choices to help keep your blood sugar levels and blood fats under control without having to live on twigs and berries."

Your body's not junk, so why feed it junk food?

Chapter Nine

Joy to the World
Entertaining

"I'm still not sure how I should handle eating out or going to parties," Mike told the educator at his next visit. "Whether I'm going out for fun or for business, I always end up way off my usual schedule. I've had several severe insulin reactions when dinner didn't arrive until after a long cocktail hour.

"I usually eat dinner at 5:30 and I take my Humalog with the meal. Most of the big dinners or parties that give me trouble don't even begin until 7, and that's usually just the cocktails. Dinner might not show up until 8 or 9 o'clock."

"Changing the time of a meal after you've taken your insulin can create problems," the educator agreed. "People who don't have diabetes have a hard time understanding that."

"Yeah, they think that having diabetes just means you can't eat sweets. At least I've found a way to make my friends understand. Now they really listen when I say it's time to get something to eat."

"What do you tell them?"

"Well, I tell them food to me is like air is to a scuba diver. A given amount of air in a tank lasts only so long, and then it's time to get another tank. Then I tell them, 'Pretend you're going diving. Your tank has exactly enough air for one hour. How important would time be to you if you were trapped on the bottom and I promised to bring you a new tank...in about an hour and a half?'"

"That's a great story. Can I use it?"

"Be my guest," Mike replied. "But first help me figure out how to handle my food and insulin when I want to eat out or go to a party."

"Well, I think the troubles you describe are probably related to two main problems, the delay in eating and the drinking of alcohol. We'll talk about both, but let's begin with your delayed meal. You really ought to have more flexibility in timing your evening meal, not just for special occasions, but to make everyday life a little less hectic too. To give you that flexibility, we'll try reducing your morning NPH. If we get that dose just right, you should be able to delay dinner for a while without having any problems. Then you would just take your Humalog when you actually eat," the educator said.

"If your morning NPH is pushing you a bit low as you wait to eat, eat a small snack—a piece of fruit, a glass of milk, or a few crackers—at your usual meal time. That should help to keep you going for at least an hour."

"But the delays are usually a lot longer than an hour when I eat out. What will happen if I delay my insulin that long?"

"Your morning NPH will last a good sixteen hours or longer. That should keep you out of trouble until you're ready to eat and take your Humalog.

"Because you're taking Humalog to cover lunch, your morning dose of NPH is much lower than it was when you were taking just two shots of NPH and Regular. One of the payoffs for taking that extra shot should be the flexibility to move your meal times around a bit without having low blood sugar levels. We'll keep working on those doses using Dynamic Insulin Dosing until you've got that freedom.

"If you were still on two shots a day, you wouldn't have that much flexibility."

"Is there anything I could have done then to handle those parties and late dinners?" he asked.

"Sure. All it would have taken was to understand when your insulins were working. Then you could have planned your attack. Because you were taking enough NPH to cover lunch, you couldn't wait until very late to eat supper. That larger dose of NPH would have lowered your blood sugar level before you got around to eating. That made sticking to your schedule very important. So, if you had been planning to eat a late supper, you could have taken your pre-dinner Regular and NPH at the usual time and then eaten your usual bedtime snack right away. That would have kept your blood sugar up until supper. The snack would have been very important to your safety.

"You should never take your insulin and then hop in the car to drive to another location without eating. If you were delayed during the trip, you could have a low blood sugar reaction.

"And remember—instead of taking your insulin at home, you could have preloaded a syringe in order to take your shot after you got to your destination. Then you could have eaten hors d'oeuvres or appetizers to approximate your usual bedtime snack. The most important thing would have been to get about the same amounts of carbohydrate foods as usual—the starches and sugars in bread, fruit, and milk—since that is what protects you from low blood sugar. If food wasn't available, you'd need to drink fruit juice or regular soda pop in place of your snack."

"What about dinner?"

"When dinner finally arrived, you would just stay as close to your normal meal pattern as possible. The whole system works because you take in approximately the same total amount of food relative to the same total amount of insulin. It's like depositing your paycheck on the first of the month, but waiting until the fifteenth to pay your bills. The checkbook balance at the end of the month is the same as if you had paid your bills on the first."

"Well, the new way sounds a lot easier, but it would have been great to have known all that before I changed insulins. Earlier you said alcohol might be part of my problem too. If I'm going to have a drink during the cocktail hour, shouldn't I decrease the size of my snack? I've got an exchange list for alcohol at home."

"Exchanging alcohol for food is an important concept for people with Type 2 diabetes, especially those who don't take insulin and are trying to eat fewer calories. The high calorie content of alcohol is their main concern. But when you're taking insulin, especially if you have Type 1 diabetes, the approach is different.

"Most people don't realize that pure alcohol alone doesn't raise the blood sugar level. In fact, on an empty stomach, alcohol can cause a severe low blood sugar reaction. Remember, the liver is like a factory that produces sugar and then stores it in its warehouse. Insulin causes the factory to decrease production of sugar and to store most of the sugar that it makes. A small amount of sugar, however, is still released into the body at a controlled rate and provides fuel for the body's activities.

"Alcohol shuts down the factory completely and locks the doors on the warehouse. No sugar can be released to the body.

So, if you're drinking alcohol and your stomach is empty, your body has no way to get more sugar after it uses up the small amount in the bloodstream. You end up getting a low blood sugar reaction. That's why it's important to eat if you're going to be drinking alcohol."

"So that's where those reactions have been coming from. I've always reduced the size of my meal when I had a cocktail or two before dinner."

"Well, now you know how to handle it, Mike. But one last thought. If you're going to drink, keep the amounts moderate—no more than one or two drinks a day. More alcohol can really interfere with the control you've been working so hard to establish."

"You know," said the young man, "some of these parties go on for hours. Two drinks won't go very far. But I guess I could switch to diet soda or sparkling water after I reach my limit."

"That's a great idea," she congratulated him. "You know, if your friends are like mine, they're probably so absorbed talking shop or having a good time that they don't really care what you're drinking anyway. The important thing is for you to find a way to have fun without creating a big change in your diabetes control."

Alcohol, Insulin, and Type 1 Diabetes*

1. If you drink, limit it to two drinks per day.

2. Your best choices are dry wines, light beers, or distilled liquor (vodka, gin, bourbon, etc.) with noncaloric mixers.

3. Eat your usual amount of food. Drinking on an empty stomach can cause severe low blood sugar reactions.

4. If possible, make sure someone in the group knows you have diabetes and how to treat a low blood sugar reaction.

5. Gasoline and alcohol don't mix. Make sure there's a designated driver in your group.

---

*If you have Type 2 diabetes and are overweight, use exchanges to fit alcoholic beverages into your meal plan. If you have Type 2 diabetes, are normal weight, and take insulin, follow the guidelines given here for Type 1 diabetes.

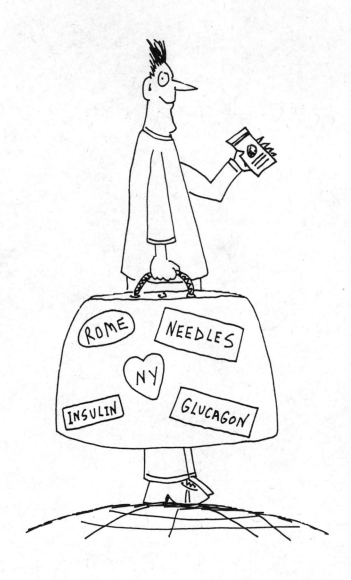

Chapter Ten

The Road to Zanzibar
Travel

"Doc," Mike said some weeks later, "I'd like to start planning for my vacation. Do you have any advice?"

"Well, first of all, travel, like the rest of life, can be a lot of fun. But it can also be trying and frustrating.

"As you make your travel plans, keep Murphy's Law in mind: 'Anything that can go wrong, will.' Applied to your vacation, Mike, that means travel is made more fun and less stressful by preparing for any foul-ups that might occur. Planning takes away their power to ruin your good time. The unexpected will still happen—but you'll be ready for it.

"The most important thing to remember is that without your insulin, your vacation would be over. If you break your last bottle of insulin at home, you know exactly where to get some more in a hurry. Away from home, it might not be that simple.

"The bag containing your insulin could be lost or damaged. It could be dropped overboard into the water or fall out of a car or bus. Or it might simply be misplaced. If any of those things happened, you wouldn't want to have all of your eggs in one basket, as they say. A separate bag with a second stash of insulin and syringes would save the day and the trip."

Mike began to see how important it was to bring a back-up supply of insulin on every trip. And he decided to keep all of his insulin in hand-carried bags from now on. Luggage compartments and car trunks can reach temperatures (both too hot and too cold) that can reduce insulin's effectiveness.

"But what if somebody walks off with my carry-on bags?" Mike asked.

"Good for you, Mike. Now you're thinking like Murphy himself! I'll give you prescriptions for your insulin, syringes, and a Glucagon Emergency Kit. Keep them in your wallet or passport case. They could save the day in a real pinch."

"Will I need to change my insulin doses to make a trip?" the young man inquired.

"It depends on the trip, Mike. If you're traveling across more than two time zones, you'll need to adjust the amounts and timing of your insulin doses. When you know your destination and your travel schedule, we can work out a transition plan. It will be based on whether you're traveling east or west and on the time difference between home and your vacation spot." (See Insulin Adjustments for Time Zone Changes, page 114.)

"How about if I limit my vacations to places either north or south of here, instead of east or west? Then we wouldn't need to adjust the insulin because of time zone changes."

"Well, that's an idea, isn't it?" chuckled the doctor.

"An idea," Mike agreed, "just not a great one. Wherever I decide to go, I'll probably be going by plane. What can go wrong?"

"Just about everything," the doctor answered. "ASSUME that planes will be late, meals will be absent or delayed, checked luggage will be lost. Carry all the diabetes supplies you might need right on the plane with you.

"Don't check anything you can't afford to be without. But never carry more than you can comfortably carry across Chicago-O'Hare at a full gallop when you have only 30 minutes between planes. At the very least, carry insulin, syringes, testing supplies, and enough food to last a day. Carrying glucagon is a good idea, too, especially if you'll be traveling with someone who knows how to use it.

"Remember the air pressure inside of the plane is lower at 35,000 feet than it is when the plane is on the ground. This causes the air inside the insulin bottles to expand. Therefore, you won't need to inject air into the bottle before drawing up your dose if you'll be taking a shot on the plane."

"How about eating on the plane?" Mike asked.

"Airline 'diabetic' meals are sometimes more trouble than they're worth. Some of them look remarkably like a 'regular' meal except for the fact that the flight attendant walks up and down the aisle with yours yelling 'Who's got the diabetic meal?' And occasionally you'll get a thoroughly ridiculous 'super diet' meal that may not have enough food for you. That can be a real problem if you're on a set insulin dose.

"Our educator recommends that you take your chances with the regular meal. Pick and choose from what's on the tray and then use your own food supplies to match your normal meal pattern. You can usually count on being able to get both regular and diet soda as well as fruit juice on flights lasting longer than 45 minutes.

"It's critical to carry food supplies so that you can take care of yourself. Having your own food will prevent a lot of stress and discomfort if your blood sugar level begins to take a nose dive while the stewardess is still chatting with the folks fifteen rows ahead. This is an important tip for every person with diabetes.

"Do you have any other questions about airline meals?

"No, not really. Although I've noticed a few times that my blood sugar levels seem to go up when I'm traveling, even if I don't eat anything out of the ordinary."

"That might not be related to food, Mike. Try walking around frequently during long flights. Also drink plenty of water or diet soda. The air is much drier at high altitudes. If you just sit there during the flight, being much less active than usual, your blood sugar may tend to rise. You urinate more when your blood sugar is high. The combination of dry air, a high blood sugar, and frequent urination can really dehydrate you. If you remember to drink enough liquids and move around occasionally, you'll arrive feeling much more energetic and your blood sugar control could be better!"

"What if I decide to go on that European vacation you mentioned on my first visit?" asked the young man.

"Sounds great to me," answered the doctor, "but there are a few extra things to keep in mind. Probably the most important is that different types and strengths of insulin are sold in other countries, compared with what you're using here. Since any change in the type, brand, or source of insulin you're using could disturb your blood sugar control, it's best to take extra insulin with you. If you have to change your insulin while on a trip, test your blood sugar more frequently and use Dynamic Insulin Dosing to get the dose corrected as quickly as possible.

"Water supplies and sanitation standards may be different from what you're used to here at home. Exotic 'bugs' in food and water could bother you. If you decide on a trip outside the country, you might find our list of Travel Tips helpful. (See page 115.)

"Once you know what to do about the safety of the food you'll be eating, there's another challenge. You'll need to figure out how the unfamiliar foods being served compare to the meals you usually eat at home.

"When you decide on a destination, ask our educator for an exchange list for the place your planning to visit. She has them for several countries. After all, we're not the only place in the world that has people with diabetes!"

"But I don't use exchanges. I just keep track of my carbohydrates," Mike explained.

"Even if you're not using an exchange meal plan, you can study the lists to learn about the foods you'll be eating at your destination. The lists can also help you identify appropriate serving sizes and the carbohydrate content of some of the unfamiliar foods.

"Finally, before leaving home, find out how to get medical care on an international trip. One way is to contact the International Association of Medical Assistance to Travelers*.

"If language will be a barrier, be sure to learn at least the phrases you would need to obtain medical care and order appropriate meals. Write those phrases down and keep the paper with you."

Mike was shaking his head. "All this preparation sounds more like getting ready for a military campaign than heading off on vacation."

"Yes, there really is quite a bit to consider. But if you pay attention to all the details, Mike, you can go anywhere your bank account will allow."

---

*International Association for Medical Assistance to Travelers, 736 Center Street, Lewiston, New York 14092. Telephone (716) 754–4883.

Insulin Adjustments for Time Zone Changes

When changing insulin doses or timing, test blood sugar every four hours to monitor the effect of your choices.

Destination Time Change: One or two time zones (hours)
Insulin Regimen: Basal/Bolus* or 2 or 3 shots per day Take unchanged doses according to home time on travel day. Begin using local time upon arising on first full day at destination.

Destination Time Change:
Three or more time zones to east (travel day shortened)
Insulin Regimen: Basal/Bolus* Decrease basal insulin by 20% on travel day. Take usual boluses with meals. Chart basal duration to determine timing on first day at destination.[†]
Insulin Regimen: 2 or 3 shots per day Decrease the day's last dose of longer-acting insulin by 20%. On the first full day at your destination, get up on "their" time and use your usual meal and insulin schedule.

Destination Time Change:
Three or more time zones to west (travel day lengthened)
Insulin Regimen: Basal/Bolus* Add a bolus for any additional meals eaten on travel day. Chart basal duration to determine timing on first day at destination.[†]
Insulin Regimen: 2 or 3 shots per day Increase the day's last dose of longer-acting insulin by 10%. Add a bolus for any additional meal(s). Chart duration of longer-acting insulin to determine timing on first day at destination.[†]

---

*Basal/Bolus therapy involves taking one or two doses of longer-acting insulin to provide a small, steady amount of insulin throughout the day and night (the "basal") and doses of either Humalog with each meal or Regular Insulin about 45 minutes before each meal (a "bolus"). This is the preferred therapy for people with type 1 diabetes who travel frequently or who are planning an extensive trip (destination more than three time zones from home).

[†]It is important to prevent both gaps in insulin coverage and significant overlaps of doses when changing time zones. NPH and Lente provide good action for up to 16 hours. Ultralente lasts up to 24 hours. If your background insulin

continued>

Travel Tips for Extensive Trips

1. If safety of the local water supply is in question:
- Drink bottled water. Carbonated beverages, beer, and wine in bottles are also safe.
- Don't use ice cubes.
- Avoid foods that are served without cooking, such as salad greens or raw fruits. Peeled fruits are OK.
- Use dental floss to clean your teeth, instead of toothpaste and the local tap water, or carry bottled water for this.

2. If you are uncertain about the food storage and preparation methods being used:
- Eat hot foods hot and cold foods cold.
- Avoid foods containing mayonnaise (spoils easily without continuous refrigeration).
- Avoid raw meat and fish (they may carry parasites).
- Avoid dairy products, including milk and ice cream, unless you know they are pasteurized.

3. Bring an adequate supply of personal toilet articles that are not predictably available in all parts of the world: facial tissues, soft toilet paper, and sanitary napkins.

4. In addition to your insulin and your prescription medication, bring supplies you will need if you should become ill on your trip:
- Medication for nausea and vomiting
- Medication for fever and pain
- Medication for diarrhea
- A thermometer

---

will be gone before morning at your destination, it is necessary to cover the gap. Ask your doctor or diabetes educator for advice about the best type and dose for your situation. If less than 12 hours will pass between your last dose on your travel day and the morning dose at your destination, ask your doctor or diabetes educator for advice. They can help you prevent overdosing due to the overlap.

5. Bring generous amounts of diabetes supplies:

- Urine strips for glucose and ketones
- Finger-stick blood sugar strips
- An extra blood glucose meter (repair or replacement may be difficult)
- Extra batteries for your meter
- Syringes

6. Know where to go for medical care. Get this information before leaving home. If an emergency arises and you cannot reach the health care providers you have identified, contact the nearest U.S. Embassy or Consulate.

When You Travel

1. **In a hand-carried bag, pack:**
   - At least one day's supply of food
   - Insulin and syringes
   - Glucagon Emergency Kit™
   - Glucose meter, strips, and lancets
   - Urine ketone test strips
   - Prescriptions
   - Other medications you use
   - List of medical facilities at your destination

2. **Take a backup supply of critical items, packed in a separate bag.**

3. **When crossing time zones, work out a transition plan for insulin with your doctor.**

4. **Before leaving home, prepare a plan for obtaining emergency medical care while you're away.**

Chapter Eleven

Up Off the Couch!
Exercise

"You know, Doc," the young man observed, "there's something else I'd like to learn about—exercise. I love to run and play tennis, but I've had so many low blood sugar problems when I exercised in the past that it didn't seem worth the trouble. It took all the fun out of it for me."

"Well, if it's not fun you probably won't do it. So let's see what we can do.

"First, it's great that you love to exercise. But, you know, there are some other good reasons to exercise besides fun.

"People who exercise regularly have a greater sense of well-being and are better able to deal with stress. Their energy level is higher, and their stamina is greater. Exercise even helps to lower blood pressure, control weight, and decrease the risk for heart disease. In fact, doctors have been recommending exercise for people with diabetes since about 600 B.C."

"I've heard all that before, Doc, but are the benefits worth the risk of low blood sugar?"

"Yes, I think they are. And I'm not the only one who thinks that. There's even an organization whose sole purpose is to encourage people with diabetes to be more active. It's the IDAA* and I'd suggest you join. You might get some helpful ideas from meeting other active people with diabetes."

"But I'm no athlete, Doc."

"That's OK, Mike. IDAA members run the gamut from people who do triathlons to those whose most strenuous activity is jumping to conclusions. Every level of sport and recreation is encouraged. But no matter what your level of activity is going to be, you need to prepare. When you do, you greatly reduce the risk of reactions and other problems. There are a few things you need to learn."

"So teach me! That's why I'm here."

"Well, the first step is picking your sport," the doctor said.

"Actually, I'd like to go back to jogging."

"That's a good choice for you. You don't have any joint or foot problems that might be stirred up by running. For people who do have those difficulties, walking or swimming would be a better way to get started. But now that you've picked your sport, let's prepare for it. I recommend that you start by getting good, well-fitting footwear as well as good, well-fitting diabetes gear."

"Well-fitting diabetes gear?"

"Yes. For example, a diabetes ID of some type, such as a bracelet or necklace, would be helpful. It can alert other people to get the proper care if you should have a problem while you're exercising. It's also important to have a Glucagon Emergency Kit along with other items to treat or prevent low blood sugar levels, such as juice, crackers, or glucose gel. Of course, if you're planning long workouts, you'll need a supply of water. And it's best to have blood sugar testing materials with you as well."

*International Diabetic Athletes Association, 1647-B West Bethany Home Road, Suite 205, Phoenix, AZ 85015. Phone (602) 433-2113.

"Are you sure you're not sending me out for an overnight camping trip, Doc? Where am I supposed to put all this stuff? I'd need to borrow the side-car off my brother's motorcycle."

"It's not that bad, Mike," the doctor laughed. "It will all fit in the same athletic bag you carry your sweats or shoes in. Most people just set the bag down in the area where they're working out."

"But how about when I run? If I'm two miles out and start to have a reaction, I'm not going to be able to make it back to some bag."

"For a moving exercise such as running or biking, use a 'runner's belt.' They're big enough to hold what you'll need including a small glucose meter."

"I understand this is all stuff I'd need if something went wrong. But what I really want to know is how to prevent problems in the first place."

"Thinking like Murphy again! You're OK," the doctor complimented him. "I was just getting to that. The first way to avoid trouble is to make sure your diabetes is in good control before you begin to exercise."

"I know that. I always check my blood sugar level before any kind of workout. If it's high, I skip the exercise."

"Do you also check for ketones before you exercise?" the doctor asked.

"Ketones? No. Why?"

"Because a high blood sugar level by itself may not necessarily be a reason to cancel a workout," the doctor answered.

"Really? My last doc told me never to exercise if my blood sugar was over 250."

"That's pretty common advice, but it misses the point. If you're feeling good and don't have ketones in your urine, you can exercise at that blood sugar level. However, if you do have ketones, that's very important information. It tells you that your body won't respond well to exercise."

"How can that be?"

"Think of the log cabin. When you have ketones in your urine, you're 'burning the furniture' instead of the wood from the woodpile. When that happens, you need to find out what the problem is and correct it before you begin to exercise. Otherwise, the exercise is just going to make matters worse."

"I don't understand."

"Remember, when you're 'burning the furniture,' your body is using fat rather than sugar for energy because it can't get sugar into the cell. This happens when there isn't enough insulin around to open the door. It can also happen when there just isn't enough blood sugar around—such as when you're having an insulin reaction.

"Since exercise increases your need for energy, exercising when you have ketones makes you 'burn the furniture' at an even faster rate. Continuing to exercise will just increase your level of ketones. As the level rises, you'll begin to feel weak and tired. In an extreme situation, all those ketones could even cause you to go into DKA (diabetic ketoacidosis)."

"So, exercising when I have ketones wouldn't be smart," Mike said. "What should I do?"

"If you find ketones when you get up in the morning and your blood sugar is in the normal or low range, test for ketones again a couple of hours after breakfast. If the ketones are gone by then, they were probably caused by a low blood sugar reaction during the night. You could go ahead with your exercise.

"If, instead, when you wake up, you find ketones and a fairly high blood sugar, say over 250, you have a real problem. Switch to your sick day schedule and skip your workouts.

When your diabetes is back under control, you can go back to your normal workouts."

"But won't I get out of shape if I miss a workout?"

"No, Mike, you don't need to exercise every day in order to stay in shape. In fact, when you exercise with ketones in the urine, you're actually tearing down muscle rather than building it up."

"Well, I don't want to do that. Will the same thing happen if I have high sugars and no ketones?"

"No. As long as there are no ketones in your urine and you feel good, go ahead and exercise. If you don't feel good, skip it. And don't fall into the trap of feeling you have to exercise to bring down a high blood sugar level."

"What do you mean?"

"Exercise for fun. Exercise for relaxation. Exercise for health. What isn't a good idea in the long run is to force yourself to exercise when your sugar is higher than you want it, just to bring it down. You might come to resent exercise as a sort of punishment. You might even stop exercising all together. You need to understand and use what you know about how exercise affects your blood sugar. But use all we've talked about to keep your blood sugars where you want them to be.

"Right now, though, your main concern is low blood sugar reactions during exercise. So let me explain how exercise decreases your need for insulin.

"Let's go back to the log cabin again. If a stiff breeze began to blow through the open door, fanning the flames in the fireplace, the fire would burn much faster than before. You would have to feed logs to the fire at a faster rate. Exercise is like the stiff breeze. It causes you to burn fuel faster and decreases your need for insulin."

"How much less insulin will I need?" Mike asked.

"That depends on how long and how hard you exercise. By checking your blood sugar before and after exercise, you can figure out how much to decrease the insulin. The reduction might be as little as 10 percent for a one-hour workout. On the other hand, it could be as much as an 80 or 90 percent drop if you were going to run a marathon.

"If you do about the same amount of activity at about the same time every day, you can adjust your usual insulin doses to that routine. But if your workout time, length or intensity changes from day to day, it takes longer to learn how to make accurate insulin adjustments for those changes. That's why, at least at the start, I recommend exercising at the same general time every day for about the same amount of time."

"When I was running regularly, it was nearly always in the morning," Mike said. "I'll probably do the same again. But how about the times when I haven't planned to exercise? My girlfriend and I like to play tennis. But I usually don't know until the afternoon if we're going to play that day or not."

"If you decide to exercise on the spur of the moment, you can't take away insulin you injected earlier in the day, but you can adjust the amount of food that's available. Eat an extra serving of fruit, starch or milk for each 30 to 45 minutes of moderate exercise. You'll do better if you eat before and during exercise to prevent a reaction, instead of waiting to eat until you feel the symptoms of a low blood sugar level."

"Sounds great. What kind of fruit or starch would you recommend?"

"Apples, bananas, and grapes should work. Try whatever you enjoy that agrees with you when you're active. A half dozen soda crackers, a small box of raisins or a small can of orange juice should also work well and are easy to carry. If your workout is going to be really hard or lengthy or if the weather's hot, concentrate on juices or soft fruits that provide fluids along with the carbohydrates."

"Is there anything else I need to do?" Mike was anxious to get started.

"Yes, as a matter of fact, there are two more things to be aware of. One is to make sure you get enough fluids when you exercise. If you lose too much water—get 'dehydrated'—your performance will suffer. It can also disrupt your diabetes control. Drink while you're exercising. Don't wait to get thirsty. About 4 to 8 ounces of fluid for each 15 minutes in your workout should keep you in good shape.

"The last thing is to make sure you get enough food, not only before and during your workout, but after it, too."

"What do you mean?" Mike asked.

"When you exercise for very long periods, your body uses up emergency sugar supplies stored in the muscles and liver. It will replace these stores later on, after you've finished exercising. Your blood sugar is likely to drop quite a bit when that happens. And if you exercise late in the day, that blood sugar drop could happen during the night. So it's important to continue to check your blood sugar after long workouts. You may need an extra snack to prevent that drop in blood sugar.

"A long workout is sort of like taking out a loan from the bank. At some point, you'll have to pay back the extra energy you used. Make sure your body has something around to pay that blood sugar 'bill' when it comes due."

Getting Set to Exercise

1. Wear diabetes ID that shows your name, address, phone number, person to contact in an emergency, and your doctor's name and phone number.

2. Get well-fitting athletic shoes that protect and support your feet. If you have trouble getting a good fit, see a podiatrist or orthopedic specialist.

3. Get a Glucagon Emergency Kit. Teach your exercise partner(s) how and when to use it.

4. Get a "runner's belt" to carry diabetes supplies.

What to take with you when you exercise:

1. Foods to prevent and treat low blood sugar
   - Glucose gel or tablets
   - Candy
   - Fruit juice or sport drink
   - Fruit or crackers

2. Diabetes ID

3. Glucagon Emergency Kit

For long workouts, also carry...

1. Water, if not available where you'll be exercising.

2. Blood testing supplies.

During exercise...

1. Check blood sugar and urine ketones before you begin.

2. Schedule workouts for the same time each day, if possible.

3. Drink plenty of fluids.

4. Eat enough food to fuel activity and cover your insulin.

5. Eat an extra serving of fruit, starch or milk for every 30 to 45 minutes of activity.

6. Learn to reduce your insulin appropriately for intense or lengthy exercise. Having too much insulin acting during exercise creates a high risk for low blood sugar reactions.

Chapter Twelve

The Gown Opens in the Back!

And Other Hazards of Same-Day Surgery

As Mike drove home from work, he turned up the radio to hear the weekend weather forecast. "Good news for you skiers," the weatherman reported. "There's a 70 percent chance of more snow this weekend to top off the heavy storms of the last week. All lifts should be open."

"Great!" Mike thought to himself. "It seems as though I've been waiting forever for the ski season to start. I'll start getting my gear together tonight and head up to the mountains this weekend."

His ski jacket and pants were easy to find because they were hanging in the back of the closet right where he'd put them last spring. A little searching turned up his hat, gloves, and long underwear on a back shelf. And his ski socks finally emerged from under the swimsuits and tennis clothes in the bottom drawer of his dresser. Mike poked his finger through a hole in the bottom of one of the socks.

"Guess I need to buy some new socks. I hope the rest of my gear is in better shape."

Now to get his skis and other equipment. Mike knew they were stored out of the way, up in the attic. He pulled the attic stairs down out of the ceiling. As he reached the top of the rickety ladder, he saw the skis leaning against the far wall, next to the poles and boots. The goggles were on a nearby shelf. "It looks like everything's in one piece," Mike thought.

Plopping the goggles on his head, he put the skis under one arm and pinned the poles to his body with the other. Then he grabbed the boots and headed for the ladder. Snow covered slopes filled his mind as he carefully juggled the load. "Why make two trips when one will get the job done?" He twisted to fit the tips of the skis through the stair opening and started down.

Unfortunately, Mike was jerked to a stop on the third step when his sleeve caught on a nail. The poles shifted as his upper body was pulled back and the skis began to slip. He dropped the boots in an effort to stop his fall, but it was too late. Mike and all of his ski gear clattered down the stairs, landing in a tangled pile on the floor. When the crashing and banging were over, Mike could tell he had a real problem. His right knee was throbbing. He'd twisted it badly in the fall.

"I can't believe I banged myself up before I even made it to the mountain. I'm going to take a lot of ribbing over this one."

Leaving the ski gear where it fell, Mike hobbled into the kitchen and made up an ice bag for his knee. He spent the rest of the night propped up on the couch watching TV.

The next morning, the knee was still stiff and swollen. "I must have really injured it," Mike decided. "I think I'd better make an appointment with that orthopedic surgeon I saw last year." He'd helped Mike a lot when he injured his ankle playing basketball.

Later that afternoon, Mike winced with pain as the doctor probed the puffy knee. "I think you might have a torn ligament, Mike, but I want to be sure. Take it easy on the knee and come back in a week for a recheck. The knee should be easier to examine by then." He wrote prescriptions for pain medication and crutches. Mike thanked him and hobbled out of the office.

A week later, on re-examination, the orthopedic surgeon confirmed his fears. "I'm afraid there is a torn ligament, Mike. I recommend arthroscopy to get you back in shape."

"What's that, Doc?" Mike asked.

"It's a type of surgery. Instead of making a big incision to open up your knee, I'll use an instrument that's like a small telescope. I'll only have to make a small cut in the skin of the knee to place it inside. It lets me examine the knee from the inside and repair it without making a large incision. You'll heal up a lot faster than you would after standard knee surgery."

"That doesn't sound too bad. Is there anything special that I need to do to get ready for this?"

"Just a few simple things, Mike. We'll do the procedure at the outpatient surgical center as same-day surgery. You'll come in, have the operation, and go home all in the same day. My nurse will give you a sheet of instructions to help you get ready."

"Will my diabetes be a problem?"

"No, Mike. Don't worry. We do this all the time with diabetic patients. Trust me. Just follow the instructions and you'll do fine."

The nurse arranged a date for the surgery and gave Mike an instruction sheet. It contained a few simple instructions. "Don't eat anything after midnight on the night before your operation. Take half your usual insulin dose on the morning of surgery. Report to the outpatient surgical center at 10:00 a.m. Your operation will be at noon. You can go home at about 5."

On the morning of surgery, a hungry Mike took half of his usual dose of insulin and drove to the outpatient surgical center. As he was checking in, he began to feel lightheaded and broke into a sweat. "I must be more nervous about this than I thought," he told himself. But as the feeling got worse, he realized he was having a low blood sugar reaction.

He hadn't eaten anything since his snack the night before, so there was no food in his stomach to counteract the insulin he'd taken earlier that morning. He could tell he was heading for trouble. He knew he should eat to treat the reaction, but he wasn't supposed to eat because of the surgery. He didn't know what to do, and panicked.

The next thing Mike knew, he was lying on the floor with a nurse kneeling next to him. "Welcome back," she said. "I gave you a shot of glucagon. Now that you're awake, I'd like you to drink this juice and eat a few crackers. You'll feel better in a few minutes."

Mike felt terrible. But as the glucagon and juice had their effect, he began to feel more normal.

A tall woman in green surgical scrubs walked over to where Mike was sitting. "Are you feeling better?" she asked.

"Not bad," Mike replied. "Can I go in for my surgery now?"

"I'm afraid not, Mike. I'm Dr. Shapiro. I was supposed to be the anesthesiologist for your operation, but now that you've had to eat something to treat that reaction, I can't put you under with anesthesia. It wouldn't be safe. You'll need to reschedule your surgery."

"Why wouldn't it be safe? I'm feeling a lot better. Honest."

"I'm glad to hear that, but the safety problem doesn't have anything to do with how you feel but rather with what's in your stomach. It's best to take anesthesia on an empty stomach. Sometimes the anesthetic can make your stomach feel queasy and cause you to throw up. If that happened after you'd eaten, you might choke on pieces of food or suck them into your lungs. So we need to reschedule this to another day when your stomach is empty."

Mike was feeling awful again, but this time it didn't have anything to do with his blood sugar level. He had planned the surgery around his work schedule. Now he'd have to juggle his appointments again. His boss wouldn't be happy.

When Mike returned to work the next day, he decided to deal with the situation head-on. He told his boss what had happened.

"You must be disappointed, Mike. I know you really need to get that knee taken care of," his boss said. "But aren't you going to just have another reaction if you do the same thing next week?"

"I thought of that too, so I'm going to see the doctor who takes care of my diabetes tomorrow. Maybe he can come up with a better plan."

The next day, Mike's doctor shook his head as the young man described what had happened to him at the surgical center. "It's a shame you had so many problems, Mike. But with the insurance companies and the government trying to control health care costs, same-day surgery centers and shortened hospital stays are being used much more. Because of this, problems such as the one you just described are occurring a lot more often than they used to. What happened to you is absolutely predictable and expected for a person with Type 1 diabetes."

"Well, why didn't the surgeon know that? He said he takes care of people with diabetes all of the time and never has problems."

"I'm sure it just didn't occur to him, Mike. Remember that a good 90 percent of the people who have diabetes have Type 2. People with Type 2 diabetes can go for a longer period of time without food than people like you with Type 1 diabetes. So they don't usually get in trouble when they don't eat anything after midnight in preparation for surgery. And because doctors and nurses successfully treat so many patients with Type 2 diabetes, they may tell you 'Don't worry, we do this all the time. Your diabetes will be fine.' They might not realize that most of the diabetic patients they have been treating had Type 2 diabetes and that there is a very big difference between Type 1 and Type 2.

"Because you have Type 1 diabetes, you need to be prepared for surgery in a very different way. We've actually had a couple of patients with Type 1 diabetes develop severe reactions while they were driving to the hospital for surgery. At least you were somewhere where you could get help when you went down for the count."

"Yeah, I guess it could have been worse. But what about next week? How do I stop it from happening again? Would it help if I took even less insulin on the morning of the surgery?"

"No, that's not the answer, Mike. Remember that you need insulin just like you need air and water. You don't breathe less air when you're getting ready for surgery, do you? If you tried to, you'd get short of breath. It's the same thing with your insulin. By taking less insulin than you really need, you run the risk of developing diabetic ketoacidosis. Without enough insulin to hold the doors of the cells open, you'll have to 'burn the furniture' in order to survive. You don't need those kind of problems on top of the stress of surgery."

"So you're saying that I should take my usual dose of insulin on the morning of surgery. But how can I do that? I passed out cold when I only took half my usual dose."

"Mike, what we need to do is admit you to the hospital on the day before your surgery to get you properly prepared."

"I'm scheduled to work that day. Don't tell me I have to take another day off work."

"No, Mike. We'll admit you right after supper so you won't have to miss any more work."

"But the hospital is going to cost more than the outpatient surgical center. Will my insurance allow that?"

"Your insurance company might say no at first. If they do, I'll explain to them that you need to be admitted because you have Type 1, not Type 2, diabetes. I've never had a problem with an insurance company once I've explained the situation to them. They allow the admission because they realize the severe problems that you can get into with Type 1 diabetes when preparing for surgery. We'll call them tomorrow and get the approval process started."

"What can you do differently in the hospital to prepare me for the surgery?"

"We'll put an IV line in a vein in your arm and run sugar water through it. That will give you the calories you need to balance your insulin while you're not eating. And I'll have the nurses do finger-stick blood sugars every few hours to make sure your blood sugar is staying in a safe range. If your blood sugar level becomes too low, we'll increase the rate of the IV to let more sugar water into your body. If your blood sugar level becomes too high, we'll decrease the rate. But either way, we'll have control."

"That makes a lot of sense. Things should go a lot better next week when we try it again. But let me ask you this. Does this mean that anytime I'm told not to eat anything after midnight that I'll need to be admitted to the hospital?"

"Yes, Mike, that's right. It's the best way to control your diabetes in that situation. In fact, whenever anyone tells you not to eat anything after midnight—whether it's for surgery or even a test—that should immediately raise a red warning flag with you. Remember that it's not the surgery or type of test that is forcing you to be admitted to the hospital. Many of these surgeries and tests can be safely done as an outpatient on individuals who don't have diabetes. The critical factor, instead, is that you need to go without food for a prolonged period of time. Any time that you attempt to go for a prolonged period of time without food, you are at an increased risk for having a low blood sugar reaction. Furthermore, in the case of surgeries, should you have a reaction and need to eat something to treat it, the surgery would probably need to be canceled. All of the time and effort that went into providing that operating room for you on that day would be wasted. So when you see those red flags go up, tell the doctor, nurse, or technician that you have Type 1 diabetes and explain what we've just talked about."

"Give me an example, Doc."

"Well, for instance, a study called an 'upper GI' is done to check people for a stomach ulcer. With this test, you swallow a substance that lines the stomach and makes any ulcers show up better on the X-ray. If there were food in the stomach, it might block the view of the stomach wall. So you'd be told not to eat after midnight in preparation for the test. For all the reasons we just discussed, it would be best to bring you into the hospital the night before. Then we could keep your diabetes under control while the test was being done.

"Another thing to remember, Mike, since we're on the subject, is that some tests involve extended preparation. For example, when X-rays are taken of the lower bowel, patients have to take medicine to clean out the bowel and drink nothing but liquids for the whole day before the X-ray is taken. This is called a bowel prep. Done in the normal way, a bowel prep would put you at great risk of having a low blood sugar reaction because the stomach and the bowel are empty."

"What would I do in that situation, Doc?"

"If you had Type 2 diabetes, Mike, you could do the bowel prep at home. We'd change your insulin dose a bit. You'd do fine. But because you have Type 1 diabetes, I'd strongly recommend that you be admitted to the hospital for the bowel prep and X-ray. We'd set up an IV line running sugar water into your arm. There would be plenty of sugar on board and you could have the prep and the test done without risking a serious low blood sugar reaction."

"Boy, it's really difficult when you have diabetes."

"Mike, I know it takes more time and money to do these things but it only becomes a problem if you don't do them, if you don't take the proper precautions. When you prepare in advance, things can go very smoothly and you can do quite well. Which leads me to one last item, your schedule. I'm going to ask your surgeon to schedule the surgery for early in the morning. That will make it much easier to manage your diabetes. We'll have time to wait until after the anesthesia has worn off to make sure you can eat without any vomiting. Then we'll send you home. I don't want you having a reaction at home after we discharge you."

Mike's doctor called the orthopedic surgeon and arranged for the admission to the hospital on the night before Mike's surgery. His case would be the first one of the day. Mike left the office still feeling pain in his knee but at least feeling relieved that his diabetes would be under control all during the surgery.

This time there were no surprises. Mike drove himself to the hospital on the evening before his surgery. The IV was started and the nurses began checking his blood sugar every few hours. He woke up in the morning feeling fine and got his morning dose of insulin. At 7:30 a.m., a nurse came to his room with a wheelchair. Mike climbed in and was rolled down to the operating room. He felt confident because everything was going so well. No reactions. No delays. No problems.

"Hi, Mike. How are you?" Mike recognized the anesthesiologist behind her surgical mask.

"Fine, Dr. Shapiro. A lot better than the last time we met."

"I'm glad to hear it, Mike. It's amazing how much difference a little planning and a bottle full of sugar water can make."

"All the difference in the world." It was the surgeon. "Well, Mike, are you ready for surgery?"

"What's to get ready, Doc? I just provide the body!"

They all laughed because now they knew better.

**Withholding food or insulin
in Type I diabetes can be dangerous.**

For this reason, many diagnostic tests and even minor surgical procedures require an admission to the hospital on the day prior to the procedure.

Section Three

And Other Things

Chapter Thirteen

Feeling Like a Frog in a Blender?

Stress

The educator was reviewing Mike's blood sugar records at one of his regular visits. She noticed a definite change in blood sugar patterns toward the end of each month and pointed it out to him.

"If you were a woman, I'd have a good idea of what's going on," she remarked. "For a lot of women, hormone changes during the menstrual cycle cause blood sugars to go out of control in a fairly predictable pattern. Changes in the insulin dose can usually compensate for that. But that obviously can't be your problem, Mike. What's up?"

"I've noticed that myself," the young man replied. "The only thing I can think of is that I work longer hours toward the end of each month. I have to complete all of my end-of-the-month paper work."

"Maybe stress is affecting your blood sugar levels."

"Stress... you may be right," he replied. "Especially when I'm waiting for the monthly sales figures to come in. My commission check depends on meeting those sales quotas."

"Well, I think we may have our answer," she agreed. "Stress and diabetes travel together a lot. One of my patients told me that having diabetes felt like being a frog in a blender—just waiting for somebody to flip the switch."

"I sure felt that way when I first came here," Mike agreed. "But now that I have a better handle on taking care of it, I think I have a lot more stress from my job than I do from my diabetes."

"Well regardless of where the stress arises, it can surely interfere with your blood sugar control." Kate went on to describe how Mike's hectic month-end schedule could be causing problems with diabetes management. "With extra demands on your time and concentration, stress may affect your blood sugar by changing your routine. When you're feeling stressed, you may not be as careful about eating and taking your insulin on time. Or maybe you eat differently because you're rushed and don't take the time to prepare your usual meals.

"Some people use more sweets and alcohol to cope during stressful periods. You might even get careless about how much insulin you're drawing up because you're worried about what the boss is going to think of your report. In short, there are a lot of ways feeling stressed can directly affect the way you manage your diabetes."

"I can see that, and I'm sure that was happening at first," Mike said. "But recently I've been more careful about food and insulin. Even so, the blood sugar levels are still a little higher and more erratic during the last week of each month than they are at other times."

The educator then described another way feeling stressed can affect blood sugar levels.

She explained that when we see life events as threats or "stressors," the body produces the so-called "stress" hormones. These hormones make fuel—sugar—available in case you need to fight or run away. That was a great response when most threats were physical—a saber-toothed tiger waiting in the bushes or a neighboring tribesman charging up behind you with a club.

"Most of the things people think of as being stressful these days—a tough supervisor, a grouchy neighbor, or stop-and-go traffic—can't be dealt with in physical terms," the educator continued. "And so the extra sugar freed up by the stress response goes unused. When this happens in a person with diabetes, the usual insulin dose just can't keep things in line. The result can be high or erratic blood sugar levels.

"Stress is an everyday part of everyone's life. Even good things like getting a promotion or buying a beautiful new car can be stressful. In fact, just being alive means you'll have stress. But it's how we respond to changes and challenges that actually determines our level of stress. 'Stressors' are usually external events, although our own thoughts can certainly be stress inducing, too. However, 'stress' itself is always an entirely internal event."

The educator used a story to illustrate:

It's Friday night in Hoboken. Old Overshoe Airlines has the last flight of the evening to Chicago. The plane is an hour late and at least 50 percent overbooked. After the ticket agents calm down most of the crowd by giving them free tickets, two sales people are left standing at the gate: Joan B. Cool and Frank Lee Steamed.

When informed she won't be able to get out of town until the "red eye" flight at 1 a.m., Joan thanks the attendant, calls her husband and sits down in the departure lounge with a new novel she bought at the airport newsstand. "I haven't had five minutes to spare all week," she says to herself. "I could use some time to myself."

Frank Lee Steamed, on the other hand, makes a loud and detailed commentary on the ticket agent's IQ and threatens never to fly Old Overshoe again. He spends the next four hours telling everyone within earshot how badly he's been treated while he pops down aspirin and antacid tablets.

Frank is definitely having a stress reaction! But Joan calmly accepts the change in plans. She even uses the extra time to relax and enjoy herself. The external event is the same. It's what Joan and Frank are saying to themselves about it that makes the event stressful or not.

"The message," said the educator, "is that things that can lead to stress are bound to happen. When they do, your diabetes control may be affected. Everybody has stress, but you can reduce its effect on your life. Take a calm look at the situation. Try to see it in a positive light. Act on your stressors, instead of letting them act on you."

Stress

1. **Recognize when you're under stress.**

2. **Identify what you're saying to yourself that makes things seem more stressful.**

3. **"Reframe" your thinking to view things in a positive light, whenever possible.**

4. **Communicate your feelings to people who add to your stress.** Be assertive.

5. **Act to meet challenges.** Plan your time. Manage your workload. Learn to say "no."

6. **Minimize the effects of stress:**
   - Approach life with a sense of humor—**laugh!**
   - Take control of your own life.
   - Make life more meaningful by seeking a satisfying role in family, work, and community.
   - Approach life with enthusiasm, seeing change as a challenge or opportunity.
   - Relax without guilt. Make time for leisure. Smell the roses.
   - Eat healthful foods and exercise regularly.
   - Get enough sleep.
   - Limit or eliminate alcohol.
   - Abstain from using tobacco and other forms of substance abuse.
   - Develop inner peace by identifying your own values and acting on them.
   - Learn to use some form of relaxation, such as deep breathing or yoga.

Caveat Emptor
(Let The Buyer Beware)
Patient Advocacy

It was a bright, cold, crisp day. The sun was shining brightly on the trees, most of which had lost their colorful leaves. It was Thanksgiving Day.

Mike was driving to his grandparent's farm in the country. As he drove through the rolling hills, he felt as if he could almost see forever. Each turn and twist in the road revealed more beautiful scenery. It was like a gourmet's feast for the eyes.

His spirits were high as he drove along happily anticipating the Thanksgiving family get-together. His grandparent's farmhouse was big and roomy and easily accommodated everyone. Not only would his parents, brother, and sister be there, but also many of his aunts, uncles, and cousins. It was always a lot of fun.

Although his grandparents were elderly now and no longer farmed the land, they still had good parties. To make it easier on them, everyone brought something to contribute to the feast. This year it was Mike's turn to do the mashed potatoes. He had the large bag of potatoes on the seat next to him. He would peel, boil, and mash them after he got to their house.

He glanced briefly at the potatoes as he thought about the upcoming culinary feast. His eyes then returned to the road and the visual feast before him.

He pushed the button to turn on the radio, looking for one of the day's many football games. The first was due to begin right after the news.

Mike drove along happily as the anchorman read the news of the day. He wasn't paying much attention until he heard the announcer say something about 'an unfortunate patient.'

Reportedly, the man had been in an auto accident the previous year. An ambulance had taken him to the nearest hospital for emergency care. The bill was almost $3,000. Unfortunately, when he submitted the bill to his insurance company, they refused to pay. The company explained to him that he was in a managed care health plan and, therefore, was only covered when receiving care in a hospital with which they had a contract. Since his injuries hadn't been life threatening, he was expected to seek out one of those hospitals to care for his injuries. If he had been treated in one of their hospitals, the managed care plan would have paid his bill.

The newscaster detailed how the patient and his wife had spoken with their family doctor about the situation. The doctor had explained that his role was that of a "gatekeeper," directing them to needed services while avoiding unnecessary treatment that would waste limited dollars. In the future, if there was an emergency, the doctor advised them to contact him first. He could make sure that they got the care that they needed and that it would be paid for.

A few weeks later, his wife had heard a loud thud coming from the bathroom. She called to her husband but got no answer. She tried without success to open the bathroom door. She could just see through the narrow opening that his unconscious body was holding it shut.

She wanted to call an ambulance immediately, but being afraid of another big medical bill, decided to call the family doctor instead. After she quickly explained, he urged her not to worry. The young man had had several seizures since the accident. This was obviously just another one. Nothing to worry about. He would wake up in a few minutes and open the door himself. "No emergency here," he assured the frightened wife. "Don't call the ambulance unless he is out for at least 30 minutes." Being extremely concerned, his wife didn't wait the half-hour. With no response from her husband, she called back, begging for permission to call an ambulance. But again, the family physician refused.

She called again in less than 15 minutes but couldn't reach the doctor. In a panic, she went ahead and called the ambulance. It arrived a couple of minutes later. The ambulance crew pushed open the door and found her husband dead. He had suffocated as he lay on the bathroom floor. He was 33 years old.

Mike felt chills travel up and down his spine as he listened to the newscaster's somber voice. The man had had a nine-year-old son and a two-year-old daughter. Thanksgiving, and the rest of the holiday season to come, would not be the same for that family.

If the doctor had told the young woman to call the ambulance at once, the young father would probably still be alive. How sad.

The football game was starting. Mike tried to concentrate on the game, but the story kept haunting him.

A few minutes later, he arrived at "Nana's house." As a toddler he couldn't say grandma, but instead used to call his grandmother Nana. Now everybody called her Nana.

As he got out of his car and reached back in for the sack of potatoes, Shelby, the huge black farm dog ran toward him, barking furiously. With a dog like Shelby around, no one ever needed to use a doorbell at Nana's. Shelby's special bark announced the arrival of every guest. No need to lock the doors either. Shelby was also a great guard dog.

Mike patted Shelby on the head and then put the sack of potatoes over his shoulder as he bounded up the porch steps and made his way towards the kitchen door. Nana, Papa, and the rest of the family were already gathered in the kitchen and greeted him with hugs. Mike's parents were on the way and were expected to arrive within the hour. Everyone bustled from sink to oven to refrigerator, each preparing a part of the coming feast. Mike threw his potatoes in the sink and started peeling.

Nana's portion of the banquet, the roast turkey, filled the house with mouth-watering smells. That smell alone could bring back Mike's memories of every Thanksgiving spent with his family over the years. The meal preparations moved along smoothly, if not quietly, and soon it was time to eat.

Mike was ready. Just before coming to the table, he had taken his Humalog. In fact, he had taken a few extra units in anticipation of the large meal he planned to enjoy. Previously, when he was on human Regular insulin, he would try to take the shot about 45 minutes before the meal. But even when he remembered to take it early, it was hard to time it exactly

As the large platters of food began to be passed around the table, Mike remembered a song that Goofy had sung in a cartoon he had seen as a child. "Turkey, lobster, sweet potato pie; Pancakes piled up 'til they reach the sky!" Goofy must have spent some time at Nana's house!

Excited chatter rose above the banging and clanging of

dishes and utensils as food moved from the serving dishes to individual plates. Then suddenly, the noise level dropped to near silence as everyone began to eat. No more noisy chatter and laughing. Just the quiet sounds of food being eagerly eaten.

When the meal ended, everyone but the dishwashing detail retired to the den. They quietly watched the last of the football games while attempting to digest the huge meal they all had just consumed.

After the last football game of the day, the CBS Evening News came on with Dan Rather. Rather was doing a special segment on "The Crisis of Medicine in America Today." As the newscaster talked, Mike was reminded of the story he had heard while driving in today. The CBS feature described how managed care was having an effect on every aspect of medical care. It was affecting medical schools, hospitals, doctors, and, most importantly, patients. All of this news about the difficulties involved in obtaining good medical care worried Mike.

The end of the year was quickly approaching, and, with it, the time to choose his health insurance plan for the coming year. He had already received forms and brochures at work that described his options. It looked like the decision wouldn't be an easy one.

At that moment, Nana came into the room with a plate full of cookies. Nobody made cookies better than Nana. And these looked like the best ever!

Mike's cousin, Joe, saw the heaping plate and yelled "Here they come!" His other cousin, Al, was the first one to grab a cookie as Nana passed the plate around. "Thanks, Nana," he said. " I always eat desserts to exercise my pancreas. You know what they say, 'if you don't use it, you lose it.' I don't want to lose my pancreas and get diabetes, so this is how I keep it in shape!"

Everyone laughed. Al had been telling the same lousy joke for the last 15 years.

Mike reached for a cookie. It was great to be with his family and enjoy Thanksgiving as they did. He had adjusted his insulin to cover that big meal and some sweets afterwards. Everything was under control. And so the day passed.

Monday came all too quickly and Mike headed back to the office. He tried to concentrate on his work, but his concerns and questions about choosing a health plan kept returning. He was still haunted by the news report about the young man who had died. It had never occurred to him before that his choice of a health plan might be such a serious decision.

When he arrived home that night, the latest issue of *US News and World Report* was waiting for him. The cover story was about HMO's and other types of managed care plans. He read it carefully. Again, there seemed to be a recurring theme of patients not receiving the care they required. "Why weren't those patients getting the care that they needed?" Mike pondered.

He knew there had always been cases of poor medical care to be found. Now it seemed that managed care had added financial issues to the causes of such problems. "How can I protect myself and make sure I get the care I need?" he wondered.

Then he remembered what one of his teachers had told him in school. "Mike, when you want to learn something about any topic, go to the library and look it up."

He couldn't get to the library until the weekend, but he did have a computer at home. He would see what he could find out online.

That night after supper, he got on his computer and began searching the Internet. He found an organization called The National Organization of Physicians Who Care at http://www.pwc.org. They offered a brochure called "Are You Thinking of Joining an...HMO?" which looked like it might be helpful, so Mike ordered one.

He began to relax as he realized that a great deal of helpful information was available. There were several Internet sites with information about what your rights are when receiving health care. Some of them also gave advice about what to do if you have a problem. It was now clear to Mike that he wasn't alone.

When Saturday came, he went to the library. As he searched through the library computer for books on health care, he came across one by Edward Annis called *Code Blue.* The author traced the current changes in medicine back to the 1700s in France. There, a man called Francois Fourier wrote about an imaginary utopian society based on centralized planning. Theoretically, it seemed to be a good idea and people tried to duplicate it in the real world. Their intentions were good, but centralized planning, with all of its regulations, just didn't work. All of the planned communities ultimately failed.

As Mike read on, he learned that centralized planning was now being used in the field of medicine. One example was the federal government's Medicare program and another was managed care.

Medicare was the government's health insurance plan for people over age 65. In an attempt to plan for their care, the government had published over 45,000 pages of rules and regulations for the system. "How can something that complicated work?" Mike wondered. "I'll bet that the only people who've ever read that stuff are the ones who wrote it.

"To keep airfares down, the government deregulated the airlines. To keep phone bills low, they deregulated the phone companies. And now, they're doing the same thing to other utilities to assure an ongoing supply of cheap energy. So, why is it that, when it comes to keeping health care costs low, they've decided to increase the amount of regulation? It just doesn't make any sense."

As Mike read on, he noted some information that might interest Nana and Papa. In 1965, when Medicare was first established, there were 15 workers for every retired Medicare recipient. In 1993, the ratio was down to four workers for every recipient. Later, Mike learned that the number had fallen to 3.3 in 1997 and was still in decline.

The cost of Medicare was skyrocketing. In order to hold down costs, the government was spending millions trying to stamp out fraud and abuse in the medical marketplace. "Even if the government could stamp out every instance of fraud and abuse," Mike mused, "would that make Medicare affordable? When there were 15 workers for each retiree, the program seemed to work. But how can it continue to work now that there are so few workers for every retiree? I wonder if it will still be there when I retire?"

As Mike's research continued, he discovered the "Sunshine Laws." Their purpose was to help patients get the information that they need to make informed decisions when choosing health care plans.

"The Sunshine Laws"

The answers to these questions should be obtained in writing from a plan salesman or other representative. Federally qualified HMOs are required by law to provide the following information to beneficiaries, but only if they are asked:

1. Does the plan have a physician incentive program that affects referral services? Is your doctor paid more for not referring you to a specialist, or less if he does?

2. What types of physician incentives does the plan use? Does the doctor get paid more if he limits the amount of medical care that he provides you?

3. Is there "stop loss" protection for higher cost cases? Is the amount of money your doctor can lose on a case unlimited or is it limited by stop loss insurance?

4. What are the results of patient satisfaction surveys conducted by the plan? Surveys that include patients who have left the plan, rather than only those who are currently enrolled, are often more informative.

As Mike reviewed the Sunshine Laws, he thought to himself, "Who would even know enough to ask these questions?"

In spite of the fact that there was a wealth of information available on the Internet, in the library, and from the federal government, Mike knew he had his work cut out for him. It obviously wasn't easy to get good medical care, but he was determined to become an educated consumer.

He remembered a Latin phrase that he once learned in school: *Caveat emptor!* Let the buyer beware!

Caveat Emptor

Healthcare could be the most important thing that you ever buy.

Helpful Resources for Consumers with Diabetes

Insurance Information

Annis, Edward, R., *Code Blue*, Regenery Gateway, Washington D.C., 1993.

Protos, J., "Ten Things Your HMO Won't Tell You," *Smart Money*, March 1996.

US Department of Health and Human Services
Health Care Financing Administration
7500 Security Blvd.
Baltimore, Maryland 21244–1850

Provides many helpful patient booklets including:
Guide to Health Insurance for People with Medicare (This is updated yearly.)

Medicare Managed Care, Publication number HCFA 02195,

Patient Advocacy Organizations

American Diabetes Association
1660 Duke Street
Alexandria, Virginia 22314
Advocate@diabetes.org

Very active in legislative advocacy and research. Provides copies of standards of medical care that identify what services patients with diabetes should receive from their doctors.

Association of American Physicians and Surgeons
1601 N. Tucson Blvd., Suite 9
Tucson, AZ 85716–3450
1–800–635–1196

Good source of information regarding the doctor-patient relationship. Publishes *The Medical Sentinel*.

Institute for Health Freedom
1155 Connecticut Ave., NW, Suite 508
Washington, D.C. 20036
(202) 429-6610

Provides information on healthcare laws and issues.

The Juvenile Diabetes Foundation
120 Wall Street
New York, NY 10005–4001
(212) 785-9500

The largest provider of non-governmental funds for diabetes research. Strong legislative advocate.

Medical Recovery Services
1–800–280–9425

Reviews hospital bills for patients.

National Organization of Physicians Who Care
10615 Perrin Beitel, Suite 201
San Antonio, TX 78217
1–800–545–9305
http://www.pwc.org

Provides patient booklet "Are You Thinking of joining an...HMO?" Maintains hotline for managed care complaints (1–800–800–5154). Provides a review service for patients who feel that they have not received needed care.

The Patient Advocacy Coalition
3801 E. Florida Ave., Suite 400
Denver, CO 80210
(303) 512-0544

Mediation specialists in health and insurance.

Society for the Education of Physicians and Patients
P.O. Box 32
Monongahela, PA 15063
(412) 929-5711

Provides useful information regarding medical insurance.

Chapter Fifteen

That'll Be $378.92

Reimbursement and Coverage for Diabetes Care

The deadline was approaching to choose a health plan for the coming year. Mike called the personnel office and made an appointment with the benefits manager. Even after reading the pamphlets for each insurance plan, there was still a lot he wasn't sure of. He hoped the benefits manager would be able to clear things up for him.

On the morning of the appointment, he walked into her office with a list of questions in one hand and his past year's medical bills in the other.

"Hi, Mike. I'm Carrie MacGuire. I understand you have some questions about the open enrollment period."

"Hi, Carrie. Thanks for seeing me. Actually my questions aren't so much about the enrollment period as about the specifics of the plans that you're offering. I want to get the right coverage, but I don't want to pay any more than I have to."

"I'm glad to see someone taking the decision seriously, Mike. Health care coverage is expensive. But it's not nearly as expensive as being without it or having the wrong kind if you have a major health problem. What did you want to know?"

Mike explained that he had two big concerns. One of them was whether his diabetes would keep him from being accepted by whatever new plan he chose. The other was how to pick the plan that gave him the best coverage for the services he needed.

"I'm in great health, Carrie. But to stay that way, I have regular visits with my doctor and diabetes educator, regular lab work, and the ongoing costs of medicine, blood testing supplies, and other things. It's pretty expensive."

"Since you're concerned about costs, you ought to be happy to know that when you're insured as part of a group, the premium is generally lower than it would be if you bought the same amount of insurance on your own. That's because the risk is spread across all members of the group."

"I know about the value of good group health insurance," Mike said. "It was a big factor when I was looking for a job. I can't imagine what people with diabetes do if they can't get insurance at work."

"Well, there are some options," Carrie replied. "People who work for small companies and those who are self-employed may be eligible for small group plans or for insurance offered by their churches or clubs, by unions and trade groups, or even alumni associations. But wherever you get your insurance, be careful when you change plans. Never let one insurance plan lapse until you've received written notice of being accepted by the new insurer. Some people call going without insurance 'going naked.' And naked is not a good way to be with health care costs at an all time high."

"How long do I have to keep the old insurance going after I've applied for the new one?" Mike asked.

"Most companies take about thirty days to deliver a new policy. But be patient. Don't cancel your old policy until you actually receive written approval from the new plan."

"I'll remember that," Mike said. "I made a list of all the health care services I've used during the last year. I'd like to compare it with the coverage provided by each of the plans you're offering. I figure that knowing both what they'll pay for and what I'll have to pay for myself will help me pick the best plan."

"That will take some time," Carrie said, "but it's the best way I know of to make a good choice. Besides looking at what is and isn't covered, also figure out what your out-of-pocket expenses are likely to be with each plan. That's not just the premium. It's also any charges the insurance company won't pay as well as the deductible. The deductible is the amount of covered expenses that you have to pay yourself each year before the insurance company begins to pay. One of our plans has no deductible, two have $500 deductibles, and one is $1,000.

"You'll also want to keep track of how much you'll have to pay after you've met the deductible for the year. Depending on the policy, that's called either the co-payment or the co-insurance. For a couple of the plans, the co-insurance is a percentage of each bill—about 20 percent. That means the insurance company pays 80 percent of a covered expense and you pay the other 20 percent. The other plans have set specific co-payments for different types of services: $5 for a prescription, $10 for an office visit, and so on. The insurance company pays the difference between the allowed charge for a service and the co-payment.

"You're trying to make a risk management decision, Mike. In risk management, you want to balance an acceptable loss (what you pay for premiums, deductibles, co-payments, and uncovered expenses) against an acceptable gain (what the insurance company pays for the services you need)."

"I think I'm going to need my calculator for this one," Mike said. "But I'm interested in more than just cost. There are a couple of other things that I'm wondering about, too. For instance, can changing plans affect where I get my care?"

"Oh, good question, Mike. It sure can. Is choosing your doctor important to you?"

"I can't tell you how important. It took me a long time to find the right doctor and I just won't change," Mike answered.

Carrie smiled. "Well, you just eliminated one of the choices. The HMO (health maintenance organization) we offer is what's called a Staff Model HMO. That means it employs its own medical staff. It doesn't pay anything toward services provided by a doctor from outside the plan. If staying with your current doctor is that high a priority, you need to look at the other plans instead. It's too bad, though. Our HMO is the cheapest plan."

"Well, cheap is great, but getting the right care is more important, as long as I can afford the difference. Which plans will let me pick my own doc?"

"Both of the regular (indemnity) insurance plans leave the choice of doctor entirely up to you. The third plan is a preferred provider organization—a PPO. That could be a good choice for you if your doctor is a member. Check the list of doctors in that plan. If your doctor is there and you decide to go with that plan, call his office before you actually sign up, just to make sure he's still a member."

"I also want to know where I can get my medications with each plan. One of my friends has to get all of his medicine through the mail. He had a lot of problems with his insulin last summer because it wasn't kept under refrigeration. Those mail trucks get pretty hot. I'd like a plan that lets me go right to the pharmacy."

"Well, that's one thing you don't have to worry about, Mike. All of the plans we're offering this year let you get your medicines from a local pharmacy. But some of them only work with certain pharmacies. So you'll want to check that out when you're reviewing the plans."

"OK, I'll put that on my list, too. It sounds as though I've got what I need to compare the plans and make a decision. Thanks for the help, Carrie."

"You're welcome, Mike. But there are a few more things you should keep in mind. Read the policies carefully to see if there are any 'exclusions'—things they don't cover—that are important to you. No health insurance plan covers everything and most only pay a part of the cost of things that are covered. But before choosing a plan, be sure that it covers the things that are important to you."

"Thanks for the warning. I made a list of the things I'm looking for and that's what I'm going to use to check out these plans before I make my choice." (See Insurance Benefits Shopping List, on the next page.)

"Good for you, Mike. And when you've made your choice, fill out the application completely and accurately. Don't try to hide the fact that you have diabetes. That would probably back-fire on you later and your claims could be denied because you withheld information."

Mike could see that his work was cut out for him. Comparing the costs and benefits of each of the plans would take some time. But when open enrollment came around, he would be ready to make a good choice.

Insurance Benefits Shopping List*

• **Office Visits:** Doctors are usually covered. Check for coverage of nurses, dietitians, podiatrists, and others you see.

• **Lab Work**

• **Diabetes Education**

• **Complete Eye Exam Yearly**

• **Medication:** Are drug choices limited? Are your drugs covered?

• **Equipment and Supplies:** Check for limits on quantities of supplies.

---

*No insurance policy covers everything. Decide which services are important to you, then "shop" the available plans to find the one that meets your needs at the best cost.

Chapter Sixteen

Summer Camp
Hormones, Adolescence, and Diabetes

The sun was shining so Mike decided to put the top down on his car for the drive to the doctor's office. It had been a while since he'd been there. His visits were less frequent now that his diabetes was in good control. He thought of his doctor visits like the oil changes on his car. Every 3,000 miles he had the oil changed and the car greased. The car dealer called it "preventive maintenance:" a check to make sure that everything was running smoothly, a way to prevent a major breakdown. Mike wouldn't skip an oil change just because his car was running well. And he wouldn't skip his doctor visits because his diabetes was in good control either. His body was at least as important as his precious convertible. As Arnold Palmer said, "It pays to keep up the old equipment."

He pulled up to the office, parked his car, and walked into the waiting room. He nodded to the receptionist and scanned the magazine rack. He liked the selection of up-to-date magazines they kept in the waiting room. What a difference from some of the other medical offices he'd been in. He settled down with an article on places to go for a summer vacation.

He did have some time off coming. Maybe he could get

away for a couple of weeks later in the summer. The sun-splashed beaches in the magazine looked inviting. But just as he was getting into the article, the nurse called his name and said that the doctor was ready to see him.

"Darn," Mike thought to himself. "Why is it that doctors who keep you waiting forever have old boring magazines and the ones who see you on time have great reading material?" He reluctantly put down the magazine and went into the examining room. The nurse weighed him and checked his blood pressure. Then the doctor came in.

"Hi, Mike," the doctor said. "How are you doing?"

"Fine, Doc," Mike replied. "No bad low blood sugar reactions since the last time I saw you. And my finger stick blood sugars are generally where we want them to be."

The doctor looked through the log book and said, "Mike, it's great to see so many of your finger sticks in the normal range. And look at your most recent lab sheet. Your glycosylated hemoglobin is only a half percent above normal. That's a big change from when we first saw you. Are you happy with the way things are going?."

"You bet, Doc. But, you know, the best part's not the numbers. It's the fact that my diabetes is finally on the back burner. I feel good, and I'm not running myself ragged to do it."

"That's great, Mike. You know, you've been on my mind lately. Diabetes Summer Camp is held during the last two weeks in July. When I heard that we needed a few more counselors, I thought of you. You've had a lot of personal experience learning how to control your diabetes. And you know what it feels like to be a teenager with diabetes. You could be a big help. Are you interested?"

"I was planning to take a vacation, Doc, but I was thinking

more along the lines of becoming a serious full-time beach bum for a while."

"Well, then, this would be perfect. The camp is right next to a small lake. It's not exactly the ocean, but it's big enough for swimming. In fact, we'll even let you use one of the high-powered camp canoes if you like. All kidding aside, Mike, I wish you'd give it some serious thought. You'd be a great role model for the kids, and I think you'd get a lot of enjoyment out of doing it."

"Sure, Doc. I'll do it," Mike said. "I can always go to the beach for a long weekend later. Where can I get all the details?"

The doctor pulled an envelope out of the desk drawer and handed it to him. "Mike" was written across the front.

"Why do I feel like a mouse that just bit down on the wrong piece of cheese?" Mike laughed.

A few weeks later, Mike pulled through the gates of the camp and parked his car. The wooded site bordered a beautiful little lake, just as the doctor had described it. But in spite of the peaceful setting, things were pretty hectic. Parents were dropping off children. Kids of all sizes were running in every direction.

"What chaos," Mike thought. There were about 100 of them. The responsibility was awesome.

Things quieted down after the parents left. The campers, counselors, and staff members all started to settle in. After he'd found the teen cabin that was to be his home for the next two weeks, Mike stowed his gear and headed over to the dining hall for supper. When he walked through the door, the first thing he saw was a teenage girl lying unconscious on the floor. One of the camp nurses was kneeling next to her, giving her a shot of glucagon. Mike glanced back at the scene several times as he filled up his tray. Within a few minutes, she started to wake up. Someone gave her a glass of apple juice and she drank it. Finally, she stood up, walked to a table and sat down.

Mike was surprised. The whole episode had caused very little excitement. The treatment was quick and effective. And the campers seemed to take it in stride. Mike carried his tray over to the table where he saw his doctor already eating.

"Did you see that?" Mike asked. "I'm really impressed at how smoothly the staff handled that."

"Have a seat, Mike," the doctor said. "That's one of the big advantages of camp. Outside of diabetes camp, a low blood sugar reaction such as that one could cause real chaos. People in other settings aren't usually so well prepared. I'm sure it was still embarrassing for her, but not like it would have been elsewhere."

Mike knew exactly what the doctor was talking about. He'd had a very low blood sugar reaction at his desk last year and someone called the paramedics. He was the talk of the office for the rest of the day. What an embarrassing situation. But here at camp, the severe low blood sugar was taken in stride because everyone knew what was happening and how to handle it. It wasn't such a big deal.

"You know, Mike, this is the first time some of these kids have met someone else with diabetes, except maybe an older aunt or uncle with Type 2 diabetes. It's great for them to meet each other. It gives them a chance to talk about what it's like to be a kid with diabetes, to give each other support, and to not feel different for a change.

"And for some of them, it's also the first time they've been away from their parents. Camp is a safe place to prove to themselves and their parents that they can take care of themselves and their diabetes."

There was a campfire after supper and the rest of the evening went smoothly. But the next day, as Mike was entering the dining hall for supper, he saw the same girl down on the ground. It was like an instant replay. The same nurse was even giving her glucagon again.

This time when she came to, Mike and the doctor asked her to join them at their table. Everyone introduced himself or herself. The girl's name was Sarah. She was 16 and at camp for the first time. She'd had diabetes for five years.

"I'm sorry to see you having so many insulin reactions," the doctor told Sarah. "I've seen that happen before though. In fact, there are almost always some kids who have extra reactions their first few days at camp. There's so much going on here. Most campers get a lot more exercise than they do at home. So they need less insulin. It usually takes a few days to find the right dose.

"But," he went on, "I'm not sure that's what's happening with you, Sarah. You don't seem to be doing a lot with the other kids. Why is that?"

"Oh, I don't know. Maybe because I really don't know anyone here," she answered.

Just then the cook arrived with the food. There was plenty of it and it smelled great. She set down platters of grilled chicken and baked potatoes and followed up with large bowls of carrots and zucchini. The salad looked fresh and colorful. Everyone was hungry after a long day of swimming and hiking. The noisy dining hall quieted down as everyone dug in and began to eat.

Well, almost everyone. Mike noticed that Sarah wasn't really eating. She'd put very little food on her plate and was barely picking at it.

"Aren't you hungry, Sarah?" Mike asked.

"No, not really." She pushed the carrots around her plate one more time.

"Gee, why are you eating so little, Sarah? I'm usually so hungry I could eat chairs after I have a bad reaction," said one of the other girls at the table.

"If you must know, I'm on a diet. I'm trying to lose some weight."

The word "diet" turned a light on in the doctor's head. He remembered seeing Sarah pick up a diet soda pop at the snack table that afternoon. She was having those severe reactions because she wasn't eating enough.

The doctor knew that this wasn't going to be an easy problem to deal with; it would undoubtedly involve dealing with Sarah's feelings about her body and how she looked. Feeling good about your own body is a big issue for teenagers. "But teenagers aren't the only ones," the doctor thought. "Considering the number of adults on weight loss diets, it's obviously a problem for some people all through their lives." He searched for the right words to discuss the problem with Sarah.

"It sounds as though dieting has thrown your insulin and food intake out of balance, Sarah. The way to stop those reactions is to get them matched up again. And you know, having to eat extra food every day to treat insulin reactions makes it hard to stick with a food plan to lose weight anyway."

"I know," she answered. "But I feel like such a dweeb sometimes because of my diabetes. I think maybe I'd get along better if I could lose a few pounds and look better. It's not fair. Other girls at school skip meals to stay thin and nothing happens to them."

"You're right. It isn't fair," the doctor answered. "Still, I'd like to tell you something you're going to have trouble believing right now: A few pounds one way or the other won't make that much difference in how other kids treat you. It'd be great if it was that easy. I'll bet if we could get people talking about it, you'd find out that there are plenty of thin and fit kids here who sometimes feel out of place, too. Try not to expect too much out of losing a few pounds.

"But if you like, I can look at your meal plan and insulin dose to help you figure out how to get more fit. Still, I have to warn you, Sarah. Eating like a bird won't get you where you want to be. You need to think about getting some exercise, too."

"OK. I guess I can give it a try," Sarah answered.

The doctor had seen other people with diabetes try to lose weight by cutting back on their insulin and allowing their blood sugars to go high. They paid a high price for losing a few pounds that way. Besides losing fat, they also lost muscle, diabetes control, and, if they ended up in diabetic ketoacidosis, sometimes a lot more.

He wondered why some people worried so much about their weight, to the point that they endangered their health. He wanted his patients to feel good and be as healthy as possible. That involved a lot more than just getting on a scale and weighing themselves every day.

"Obviously I can't solve this problem single-handedly," he thought as he talked with Sarah for a few more minutes. But the meal was ending and it was time to get ready for the evening campfire. Tomorrow was another day and maybe in the coming week he'd be able to discuss it with her some more, maybe even involve her parents. Maybe not.

On Tuesday morning Mike was scheduled to help Kate at the blood-testing station before breakfast. Several campers had already come and gone when Lucy, one of the junior counselors, arrived. When she looked up after completing the test, her eyes were filled with tears.

"What's wrong, Lucy?" the educator asked. "Is there anything I can do to help?"

"I don't think so, Kate. It's hopeless. No matter what I do anymore, my blood sugar tests are a mess. And my folks are really upset. They think I'm eating junk or something. But I'm really not. I'm doing the same things I've always done, but instead of my blood sugar levels being where they should be, they're all over the place. I thought they'd get better up here because of all the exercise, but it's just the same."

"That must be so frustrating for you, Lucy. Do you mind my asking how old you are?"

"Almost 14," she offered.

"I thought so. Lucy, have you heard about how your hormones go on the march when you become a teenager?"

"Yeah, sure. I know all about puberty, periods, and pimples!"

"Well, the same hormones that do all those things for you and complicate your life can also make it really difficult to control your diabetes. I think that may be at least part of the reason for the high blood sugar levels that are upsetting you and your parents so much. Almost every teenager with diabetes has the same problem, to one extent or another. I have an article about this that you might like to read and show to your parents. It won't help your blood sugar levels, but it may take some of the pressure and frustration off you and your folks. And talk to your doctor about this the next time you see her. She may want to change your target blood sugar levels until your hormones stabilize."

"Thanks, Kate. Can I get the article from you this afternoon?"

"Sure, Lucy. Come over to my office in the community hall after lunch."

After the last of the campers finished their blood tests and went in to the dining hall, Mike turned to the educator. "Where were you when I was a teenager, Kate? There were times when a little information like that sure could have smoothed things out for me. You did a nice thing for Lucy."

"Thanks, Mike. That's one of the big enjoyments I get out of my job. Sometimes you get to do a nice thing. Are you enjoying being a counselor?"

"To be honest, I had my doubts at first," he replied. "But now I'm really getting to like it. Let's go get some breakfast."

The next day Mike was on the soccer field. It was the Reds against the Blues. Mike was on the Blue team. He'd played soccer in high school and it was great to be playing again. The teams were evenly matched, so possession of the ball turned over from one team to the other very quickly. Mike was running up and down the field continuously. It was demanding. But he was in shape and able to do it. Then he noticed that one of his teammates wasn't doing as well.

His name was Tom. He was 15 and the whole team knew how much he wanted to play on his school's varsity soccer team. Mike had to admit the kid was determined. He worked out every day trying to build himself up. But he was a skinny youngster and didn't seem to have much strength or staying power. And he was always thirsty. At first, Mike thought the thirst was being caused by the summer sun, but then he realized no one else was drinking as much as Tom. Mike was concerned and suggested that the boy see the doctor at morning sick call.

Tom reported to sick call right after breakfast the next morning. The nurse measured his height and weight and did a finger stick blood sugar. It was 310. Even though Tom thought that the blood sugar was high because he'd just eaten breakfast, the doctor was suspicious. He had the nurse check Tom's urine for ketones. The test was positive. There were ketones in Tom's urine.

"Tom," the doctor said, "Mike has told me how much you love soccer. He said that you're planning to try out for your school's team in the fall."

"That's right, Doc."

"But he also tells me you have trouble keeping up with the other boys."

"I do my best, Doc. I try hard and I exercise every day. I'll get better. The coach says all I really need is desire, and I've sure got that."

"That kind of motivation is great to see, Tom. But I think your diabetes may be holding you back from reaching your goal. Look at these height and weight tables for your age. According to the chart your doctor sent along, it looks like you haven't been growing as much as you should be lately. You used to be relatively big for your age. Now, suddenly, you're on the small side."

"But Doc, how can that be? My father's tall and all my brothers are big, too. Won't I be big like them?"

"Not if your diabetes stays out of control."

"What do you mean?"

"Tom, when your diabetes is way out of control, your body can't grow and develop as it should. Right now you're spilling ketones in the urine and your blood sugar is quite high. When that's going on, calories from some of the food you eat are lost in your urine instead of being used to build up your body.

"You're a teenager. About now you should be having what we call a growth spurt—a time when you move pretty rapidly from your kid-size body into your adult size. But that won't happen with your diabetes out of control. You'll only reach your full potential size if your blood sugar levels stay in better control. If you don't keep them under better control, you may end up shorter and with less muscle than you should have."

"But, Doc, I exercise all the time. Won't that build up my body?"

"Only if your diabetes is well managed, Tom. When you build a house, you have to put it on a solid foundation. If the foundation is weak, the entire house will crumble. It's the same thing with your body. Healthy foods and good diabetes control make up the foundation you need to build a stronger body. Without that foundation, all the exercise in the world won't give you the strength and endurance you want. When diabetes is out of control, your body just can't build muscle mass."

"I never knew that. Okay, Doc, what do I need to do?"

"First, I'm going to increase your insulin to get rid of those ketones. Then let's start getting some blood sugar readings. By the time you go home, things should be looking a lot better."

As soon as the ketones cleared, Tom noticed how much more energy he had. And he was playing better. His weight was even up a few pounds by the end of the week. He'd been trying to gain weight all spring without success. Now that he understood what was going on, he could see that he needed to make diabetes control an important part of his training program.

At the soccer game on Friday, Tom waved at Mike. "Thanks for sending me to see the doctor, Mike. I think it's going to make a big difference."

"That's great news. You're looking a lot stronger out there,

Tom. Let me know when you make the team. I'd love to come and watch you play."

After the game, Mike walked back toward his cabin. He wished that things were going as well for Brian as they were for Tom. Brian was one of the boys in his cabin. He was 12 years old and an only child. Mike had watched the boy and overheard some talk in the cabin that worried him. It seemed that Brian used his diabetes to get what he wanted from his parents. He'd found out that if he made his blood sugar levels go out of control, he could get just about anything he wanted.

He bragged to the other boys about how he sometimes skipped a meal to bring on a bad reaction. At other times he ate extra sweets or even squirted his insulin down the bathroom drain to send his blood sugar so high it didn't even register on his meter.

Mike remembered doing some pretty outrageous things himself when he was about Brian's age. Life had seemed so unfair. But his parents had been strict about certain things. They even "kept him company" while he took his shots for a while. Things had eventually straightened out. He hoped that Brian would be as lucky.

Mike got busy after supper preparing for the hiking contest that was on the schedule for the next morning. Each hiker would get a whistle, a map of the course through the woods that he'd laid out, and a compass. The first one to complete the course would get the grand prize—no kitchen duty for two days.

Saturday morning dawned warm and beautiful. Seventeen hikers set off down the course. Mike was waiting at the finish line when the first hiker returned to camp at mid-morning. It was Brian. Mike was still shaking the young man's hand when one of the other counselors came down the trail out of the woods.

"Brian, I'm sorry," she said, "but I saw you leave the course and take a short cut. I won't say anything in front of the others, but I have to disqualify you."

Brian glared at her and Mike. "It's just a stupid kid's game anyway. I could've won if I'd wanted to. You'll be sorry you treated me like this." Brian stomped off in the direction of the cabin and remained out of sight for the rest of the afternoon.

Later, he ignored Mike's invitation to sit with him at dinner. Instead, he walked to an empty table near the door to the kitchen. The next time Mike saw Brian, the boy was sitting on a rock at the far edge of the evening campfire gathering. He walked over and stood next to him.

"Didn't see you eating much dinner, Brian."

"So what," the boy replied.

"Planning on having a reaction here pretty soon?"

"Soon enough."

"Brian, you're not at home. You're at camp. There are rules here. If you don't follow them, there are consequences. At home, taking out your anger by not eating may shake your parents up and cause a lot of excitement. Around here all it'll get you is a few dirty looks and a one-way ticket back home. I'd hate to see that happen. You've got a great sense of humor. You brought the house down at lunch yesterday. But your behavior cut you off from all the fun today. Take some advice from somebody who's been there. Stop using your diabetes like a club on the people around you. It's dangerous. And it doesn't do much for your popularity either."

The next morning Mike went over to sick call to talk to the doctor about Brian.

"I'm not sure I did the right thing, Doc."

"Oh, I think you did just fine, Mike. You showed Brian that you care and maybe what you said will make him reconsider what he's doing. Being a teenager is a tough job, even if you don't have diabetes. There's so much change. Your body turns into somebody else's. Your hormones go on a rampage. You try to figure out who you are and how you fit in with the rest of the world. A lot of youngsters with diabetes use their condition to act out all that turmoil. In some ways, it's just another situation they might use to figure out who they are. It's something like wearing trendy clothes or an extreme hair style, listening to loud music, or having friends who drive their parents crazy. But it's different from those things, too, because it can be a lot more dangerous.

"I try to encourage my teenage patients to find safer ways to establish their identity than skipping meals or insulin shots or writing down blood sugar tests they never did. But those things still happen sometimes. Parents need to recognize, without laying blame, the potential for this kind of behavior. But they still need to set some guidelines. When that happens, both the kids and the parents will probably survive adolescence."

"I remember the doctor I used to see when I was a teenager," Mike said. "He told me, 'You've got to be a teenager, Mike, but try to leave your diabetes out of it as much as you can. Do it the way your friends do. Dye your hair blue if you want, but, for goodness sake, don't skip your insulin!'"

"He sounds like a wise man. But, Mike, do me a favor. Don't spread that advice around too much up here. I don't want to have to explain a lot of blue hair to irate parents."

"OK, Doc. I'll try to keep it to myself. By the way, thanks for luring me up here. It's been great."

Being a teenager is hard. Having diabetes makes it harder.

Chapter Seventeen

What Can We Learn from the Black Box?
Research

"You know, Doc, my sister is worried she might get diabetes like I did."

"It's not like the flu, Mike. She can't catch it from you."

"Oh, she knows that, but she's worried because we have diabetes in the family. She thinks she'll get it too. She even borrows my meter once in a while to test her blood sugar, to make sure she doesn't have it yet."

"That's understandable. Fear of developing diabetes is a common worry in the families of people who already have it. Brothers and sisters worry they'll get the disease. Parents worry their other children will develop diabetes. And the people who actually have it worry about whether they should have children themselves for fear their kids may end up with diabetes, too. So your sister's not alone in her concerns."

"But tell her there are better tests than a finger-stick blood sugar to let her know what's going on."

"What tests are those?"

"They're called immunologic tests. They test for substances in the blood such as the islet-cell, insulin, and GAD antibodies."

"What does immunologic mean?"

"The body's defense system is called the immune system. It protects the body against infection. These tests measure it. That's why they are called immunologic tests."

"How do they work?"

"Well, Mike, we've talked about the fact that you developed Type 1 diabetes when the beta cells in your pancreas were destroyed. We know the body's own immune system is involved in this somehow. But we don't know yet exactly what happens.

"When the immune system is destroying the beta cells, antibodies show up in the bloodstream. The antibodies are there long before the blood sugar level shoots up. That's one of the reasons they are a better test for your sister than a finger-stick blood sugar. Their presence in the bloodstream is an early sign that Type 1 diabetes has begun to develop. Research is being done in order to understand them better. The islet-cell autoantibody test was the first test of this kind to be made widely available."

"So these tests can tell years in advance if someone is likely to get diabetes?"

"Right."

"Well, excuse me, Doc, but that sounds like a really depressing piece of news. What possible good can come out of knowing for years that you're going to end up taking insulin and testing your blood someday?"

"I'm sure it sounds that way at first, Mike. But it's actually critical information. It's important, not only to the person who has the test done, but also to everyone who might develop Type 1 diabetes in the future. Those immunologic tests are like the flight data recorder on a commercial airliner—that thing they call the 'Black Box.'"

"Doc, you sure have a lot of stories about flying and air-planes. Are you a frustrated pilot?"

"Well, now you know my secret, Mike. But let me explain what I mean. When an airplane goes down, investigators show up at the crash site searching for clues. Their first job is to find the Black Box. Everything that happened in the final moments of the flight is recorded in that box. They use that information to reconstruct the flight and pinpoint the exact cause of the crash. Their goal is to prevent future accidents."

"So you're saying the beta cells of a person developing Type 1 diabetes are like a plane headed for a crash?"

"Yes, in a way, they are. And we hope that by improving our knowledge of how diabetes develops, we'll be able to fig-ure out how to prevent it in the future."

"Now that's information that would really interest my sis-ter. How can screening with these immunologic tests help?"

"Before the tests for the antibodies were available, researchers were limited to examining the aftermath of the 'crash.' It was like trying to figure out what had caused a plane to crash in the days before the Black Box. Without a Black Box, the only sources of information were the pieces on the ground. Specific information about what happened just before the crash wasn't available until the development of the Black Box. It provides a wealth of information, including the airplane's final course, attitude, and speed. Knowing what occurred just before the crash helps the investigators figure out how to prevent the same thing from happening again.

"By monitoring changes in these various antibodies and in blood insulin levels, diabetes researchers have begun to build an accurate picture of the events that lead up to the 'crash' of the beta cell. Now they're no longer working with just the pieces on the ground. In fact, they can now identify people who will develop Type 1 diabetes years before their symptoms begin—before their blood sugar levels even begin to rise. Researchers can then follow these people to find out what goes wrong and try to figure out a way to prevent the crash of the beta cell.

"Immunologic testing has already given us a very important piece of information—namely, that Type 1 diabetes develops over a period of several years."

"Not for me, Doc! My diabetes came on suddenly. One day I was perfectly fine, doing everything I'd always done. Then, almost overnight, I was drinking everything I could get my hands on and urinating constantly—eating everything in sight but losing weight. That change only took a couple of weeks, not years."

"I know what you're saying, Mike. I was actually taught in medical school that Type 1 diabetes develops very rapidly. But it's not true. Although the symptoms come on suddenly, the disease itself actually develops over a long period of time. Some people have gone as long as ten years from the time they were first found to have islet-cell antibodies until they developed diabetes. They felt fine until right before the diagnosis was made, but their ability to make insulin had been failing with every year that passed."

"How could they have normal blood sugar levels and feel fine if they were making less insulin?"

"We think it's because the body has a relatively huge supply of beta cells, compared with the need for insulin. Researchers believe that as much as 90 percent of the beta cell mass has to be destroyed before blood sugar levels begin to rise. To look at it another way, once the blood sugar is abnormal, almost all of the beta cells have already been destroyed."

"So you think my sister should have these immunologic tests done?"*

"Yes, Mike, I do. Using information from enough people like your sister—people who have brothers, sisters, parents, or children with Type 1 diabetes—researchers may be able to understand the whole process of beta cell destruction and eventually come up with a way to prevent it.

"Right now, a study by the National Institutes of Health is underway. It's a huge study. Over 60,000 people have been screened so far. People who are identified as being at the highest risk for developing Type 1 diabetes are being treated medically in an attempt to stop the diabetes. In the next few years, we should know if they've been successful. I believe that even if the treatment they're trying now doesn't work out, ultimately they'll find an approach that does."

"Why do you say that?"

"Because researchers have found animals that develop Type 1 diabetes just as humans do. Two of the animals are the NOD mouse and the BB rat.

"The researchers have found treatments that actually stop diabetes in these animals. If they can do it in animals, they should eventually find a way to apply that knowledge to stop diabetes in humans too."

"Wow, that's incredible," said Mike.

---

*Various research centers, including the Joslin Diabetes Center in Boston, Massachusetts, (1-800-242-5836), and the Barbara Davis Center for Childhood Diseases, University of Colorado in Denver (303-315-8796), and others can perform immunologic testing for relatives of persons with Type 1 diabetes from throughout the country.

The National Institutes of Health is conducting the DPT-1 (Diabetes Prevention Trial—Type 1) in which eligible relatives of people with Type 1 diabetes are tested for various immunologic factors free of charge. Eligible individuals are then offered the option to participate in the study. The research is evaluating various medical treatments for their possible effectiveness in preventing the onset of Type 1 diabetes. For more information contact: Diabetes Prevention Trial (DPT-1), P.O. Box 016960 (D-110), Miami, Florida 33101 (1-800-425-8361).

"Researchers are even looking into the development of vaccines to stop Type 1 diabetes. Wouldn't that be great?

"Mike, I really think that someday Type 1 diabetes will be like polio. Prior to the 1950s and the discovery of the vaccines that stopped polio, it was a dreaded disease. Now, because everyone is vaccinated, you hardly ever hear about polio any more.

"Sure, Doc, but what about me? I already have diabetes. Will those vaccines help me?"

"Not directly, Mike, but possibly indirectly."

"What do you mean?"

"Some of the information that has come from the efforts to prevent diabetes is now being applied to pancreatic transplants, to treat people like you who already have it.

"In the past, pancreatic transplants often failed. The body's immune system, which had destroyed the original pancreas, attacked the new pancreas in the same way. After all that effort, the diabetes would return.

"Now it's possible to blunt the attack of the immune system on the transplanted pancreas. This significantly increases the chances that it will continue to work.

"In fact, we are now recommending that any diabetic patient who is about to undergo a kidney transplant also consider having a pancreatic transplant at the same time. We recommend this because the medicines that are used to protect the new kidney are also helpful in protecting the new pancreas. So, it's worth a try."

"But my kidneys are working fine. Are there any other things that the researchers are working on that could help me?"

"Yes, Mike. A number of research centers are trying to develop a glucose meter that doesn't require pricking the finger. A meter like that would be painless."

"Doc, that would be great. Pricking my finger hurts more than giving the insulin shot. Maybe, if getting a blood sugar value didn't hurt, I could do it more often. More information could help me get even better control."

"Yes, Mike, and some day it might even be possible to have a painless glucose meter feed that data into an insulin pump which would then give your body the right amount of insulin."

"Sort of an artificial pancreas, right?"

"Yes, and in fact, researchers are also working on another type of artificial pancreas that uses actual beta cells to produce insulin. They're placing them in a protected capsule that may allow insulin to seep out into the body without allowing the immunologic system to come in and destroy the cells.

"But right now, Mike, I want to be sure that we keep your diabetes in the best control possible so that when these research breakthroughs come, you'll be ready for them."

"Sounds good to me, Doc. I'll do my best."

Research done today might stop diabetes tomorrow.

Chapter Eighteen

Is There a History of Death in Your Family?

Complications

It was Sunday evening. The young man was walking along the beach to watch the sunset. A few lazy clouds hung motionless near the horizon as the yellow glare of the afternoon sun softened to a pink and golden glow.

A familiar form shifted position on the rocks near the water's edge. It was Mike's doctor. He sat gazing silently across the bay at the setting sun.

"Hi, Doc."

"Hi, Mike."

"What are you up to?" Mike asked.

"Oh, just sitting here thinking."

"About what?"

"Life, actually. Sometimes I come down here to think about life. It helps me keep things in perspective."

"Perspective?"

"Well, I see a lot of people in the course of a day—often when things aren't going too well for them. They're sick and they're worried or scared. Or someone they care about is sick. And sometimes they share their deepest thoughts and concerns with me. I get to see a side of life that most people don't."

"I imagine that's pretty hard to take sometimes."

"Yes, it is. But on the other hand, it's taught me a lot."

"Like what?" Mike asked.

"Like how people respond when life throws them a curve. I've seen people respond in very different ways."

"I can tell you how I responded to being told I had diabetes. I got depressed. Actually I was scared at first. And then I got angry. Since then I've been mostly frustrated. It's been a lot better since I've learned to take care of myself, but it still gets me down. Especially when I think about the long-term picture."

"I understand," the doctor replied. "A lot of my patients have told me similar stories. But what's really amazing to me—what really makes me think about my own outlook on life—is how some of my patients have actually turned that situation around to their own advantage."

"Give me a break, Doc. You can't tell me there's anything good about having diabetes. It's a royal pain."

"Yeah, there's no doubt diabetes is a hard hand to play. But some people seem to play it very well. They end up eating better and getting more exercise than they did before. They live each day to the fullest. It's as if, for some people, the diabetes is a constant reminder to push ahead and live well. And then there are others who seem to see diabetes as something that holds them back."

"It's a good point, Doc. Nobody's life is perfect. You do have to play the hand you're dealt. After all, it's the only one you have. But every time I pick up a book about diabetes, I'm reminded of those long-term complications. I feel as if the clock is running, and it's just a matter of time until the complications begin. I ask myself, 'When will my eyes start to bother me? How long will my kidneys last?' Some of the numbers are frightening."

"This is something I discuss with my patients quite often," the doctor said. "It's an area where perspective is really important. To put your concern about complications in perspective, we need to talk about two things: one is the way diabetes care has changed in the last few years and the other is whether there is a history of death in your family."

"What do you mean?"

"Well, if you go back as far as 1921, before insulin was available, a diagnosis of Type 1 diabetes meant death in six months to two years. But then insulin became available and the book had to be rewritten. With insulin, people survived. In fact, they survived long enough to develop the complications we worry so much about today.

"Those frightening numbers you talked about earlier—the ones quoted as the chance you'll develop a certain complication in a given number of years—were developed between the 1920s and the 1980s, a period when the standard of diabetes management was very different from what it is today.

"Now, patients are actively involved in their own care and we have a lot of technical advances at our fingertips. We can achieve much better blood sugar control than was possible at the time those statistics were compiled. And we now know, due to the results of the Diabetes Control and Complications Trial, that good blood sugar control does make a difference. Together with control of cholesterol and blood pressure, better blood sugar control can help prevent the tissue damage that leads to diabetes complications. I think we're going to have to rewrite the book again."

"That makes sense to me, Doc. But what do you mean, 'Whether there is a history of death in my family?' Everyone has a history of death in their family."

"Exactly!" the doctor answered. "Everyone is going to die.

All of your ancestors have done it, and you're going to do it, too. And the same would be true even if you didn't have diabetes. Everyone will die of something. And all of us—whether we have diabetes or not—have some tendency to develop health problems as we get older. How much of a tendency—or 'risk'—we have varies.

"One of the things that affects our risk for health problems is how well we did picking our parents—in other words, our genetic tendencies. If we picked parents who made the mistake of dying at a young age of heart disease, our risk is greater than if we'd been smart enough to pick parents who lived to a ripe old age.

"Of course, I'm kidding you a bit, but the point is this: We all have some degree of risk for developing health problems as we go through life. A portion of that risk can't be controlled. Diabetes adds to the risk, but it doesn't make health problems a certainty.

"On the other hand, there are things that influence risk that we do have control over: eating well, staying physically active, avoiding smoking and substance abuse, and keeping blood pressure and blood sugar levels under control. These are things we can do to minimize whatever risk we have inherited from our parents or acquired through developing diabetes."

"I think you're right," replied the young man. "I guess whether we have diabetes or not, we only have so much tread on our tires. And it's a matter of trying to get the most mileage possible out of the tread we've got."

"Now you're telling stories, too," the doctor observed. "Think you've spent too much time with us?"

"Not really," Mike replied. "Sometimes the stories help me see things more clearly. They get the point across and make the facts easier to remember."

The doctor motioned to Mike and they began walking back up the beach. "It's too late now to go back and pick different parents, Mike. And you can't get rid of your diabetes just yet either—although you may see that happen in your lifetime. So, as the old philosopher once said, 'A wise man accepts what he can't change.'

"But the things you can change—what you eat; how much you exercise; how well you control your blood sugar, blood pressure, and cholesterol; whether or not you smoke; whether or not you wear your seat belt, and so on—are well worth the effort. They can make a difference. And that's just as true for people who don't have diabetes as it is for those who do.

"Remember your family not only has a history of death, it also has a history of life!

"Go out and live it well!"

There is hope. You have control!

Index

A

ACE inhibitors, 51
adolescents
    diabetes summer camp, 169–180
    dieting, 172–173
    growth spurts and, 176–177
    hormones and, 174–175
    using diabetes to act out,
        178–180
adult onset diabetes, 10
alcohol
    effect on blood sugar level,
        104–105
    tips for, 106
American Diabetes Association, 156
Annis, Edward, 153
arthroscopy, 131
artificial pancreas, 189
artificial sweeteners, 95–96
Association of American Physicians
    and Surgeons, 156
asymptomatic reaction, 59–60

B

bedtime snack, 36, 38–39
beta cells, 184
    developing diabetes and, 184, 186
blood glucose meters, home
    accuracy of, 60
blood pressure
    checking, 52
blood sugar action point, 25

blood sugar level
    alcohol and, 104–105
    bad, 47–48
    exercise, 121, 123
    guilt and, 48
    high and Dynamic Insulin Dosing
        Guidelines, 25
    low and Dynamic Insulin Dosing
        Guidelines, 26
    stress and, 141–144
    unexplained high, 47
blood sugar test
    fasting, 49
    finger-stick blood sugar, 43–45
    importance of doing several dur-
        ing day, 43–44, 45
    lightening up on, 46–47
    on sick days, 79
    timing of, 44
bowel prep, 136–137
breakfast cereal
    picking, 93–95

C

carbohydrates
    carbohydrate intake and insulin
        dose, 36–37
    importance of counting, 89
    keeping track of, 32
    Nutrition Facts label and, 93

cereal
  picking, 93–95
cholesterol
  checking, 52
Code Blue (Annis), 153
Compazine tablets, 78
complications
  changes in diabetes care and,
    193–195
  history of death in family, 193
cough medicines
  sugar-free, 82

D

decongestants
  sugar-free, 82
dehydration
  exercise and, 125
  sick days and, 77–78
Diabetes Control and Complications Trial, 5–6
diabetes educator
  job of, 29
diabetes identification, 64, 66
  exercise and, 120
diabetes summer camp, 169–180
  benefits of, 170
diabetic ketoacidosis
  defined, 71
  exercising with high ketone level,
    122
diagnostic tests
  that require prolonged periods
    without food, 136–137
dietetic foods, 98
dieting, 172–173
doctors
  health maintenance organization
    and choosing, 162
  importance of choosing a good,
    4–7
double-voided urine test, 79–80
Dynamic Insulin Dosing Guidelines,
  16
  defined, 24
  high blood sugar, 25
  insulin activity, 24
  low blood sugar levels, 26
  tips for, 27

E

entertaining, 101–106
  alcohol and, 104–106
  delayed meals and, 102–104
exercise, 119–127
  benefits of, 119
  blood sugar level before starting,
    121, 123
  checking blood sugar after long,
    125
  dehydration and, 125
  eating before, 124–125
  equipment for, 120–121
  insulin need and, 123–124
  International Diabetic Athletes
    Association, 120
  ketone level before start,
    121–123
  lowering blood sugar level by,
    123
  summary of tips for, 126–127
eyes
  importance of testing, 51–52

F

fasting blood sugar test, 49
fat
  burning and ketones, 71
fats
  hydrogenated, 97
  monounsaturated, 97
  polyunsaturated, 97
  saturated, 96, 97
feet
  checking, 52
finger-stick blood sugar
  devices for, 45
  reducing discomfort of, 44–45
fluids
  exercise and, 125
  intake of, on sick days, 77–78
fruit juice
  hypoglycemia and, 58, 65

G

gestational diabetes, 10
  characteristics of, 11–12
glucagon, 62–63
  limitations of, 63
  mechanism of, 62
  reasons for using, 62–63

Glucagon Emergency Kit, 64, 66
  sick days and, 78
glucose gel/tablets
  hypoglycemia and, 58, 65
glycosylated hemoglobin
  defined, 50–51
granola bars, 91

━━━H
headaches
  hypoglycemia and, 61–62
health care
  changing insurance plans, 160
  choosing your doctor, 162
  co-payments for, 161
  deductibles for, 161
  exclusions, 163
  insurance benefits shopping list,
    164
  insurance information, 156
  options for, 160
health maintenance organizations
  choosing your doctor and, 162
  concerns about, 148, 152, 153
  Sunshine Laws, 155
hormones
  adolescents and, 174–175
  low blood sugar and, 56
  stress and, 142–143
Humalog insulin, 18
  activity of, 24
  high blood sugar guidelines, 25
  Humalog before meals and NPH
    insulin in a.m., 34
  low blood sugar guidelines, 26
  timing of eating and, 19–22, 37–38
hyperglycemia
  exercising to lower blood sugar
    level, 123
hypoglycemia, 55–66. See also low
    blood sugar
  alcohol and, 104–105
  asymptomatic reaction, 59–60
  danger of prolonged period with-
    out food, 135–138
  first step for, quick-acting sugars,
    58, 65
  glucagon and, 62–63
  headaches and, 61–62
  hormone release and, 56
  range for treating, 60–61

  same-day surgery and danger of,
    135–138
  second step for, log food, 58–59
  summary of steps for, 65–66
  symptoms of, 56–57
  taking morning insulin at night by
    mistake, 64
  unconscious state and, 63

━━━I
immunologic tests, 183–187
ingredient list
  breakfast cereal, 93–95
  granola bars, 91
  order of ingredients on, 89–90
  peanut butter, 90–91
  refined sugar and, 90
  Total Carbohydrate, 93
Institute for Health Freedom, 157
insulin, 15–19
  activity of common, 24
  adjusting for delayed meals,
    102–104
  back-up supply and travel,
    109–110
  carbohydrate intake and insulin
    dose, 36–37
  combining different types, 17–18
  exercise and need for, 123–124
  fitting needs of, 15–16
  Humalog, 18, 19–22
  insulin supplements for sick days,
    75
  intermediate-acting, 17, 18
  Lente, 18
  NPH, 18
  Regular, 17–18
  role of, 15
  short-acting, 17–18
  sick days and amount taken
    during, 72, 74
  static dosing of, 16
  taking morning insulin at night by
    mistake, 64
  time zone change and adjust-
    ments for, 110, 113–114
  timing with eating, 19, 37–38
insulin-pump, 189
insurance information
  for consumers with diabetes, 156
intermediate-acting insulin, 17, 18

International Association of Medical
Assistance to Travelers, 113
International Diabetic Athletes
Association, 120
islet-cell antibodies, 183–186

J

juvenile diabetes, 10
Juvenile Diabetes Foundation, 157

K

ketones, 53
burning fat and, 71
danger of high levels of, 71
defined, 48
exercise and level of before,
121–123
morning urine tests for, 53
sick days and insulin supply, 75
kidneys
testing of, 51, 52

L

Lente insulin, 18
activity of, 24
high blood sugar guidelines, 25
low blood sugar guidelines, 26
liver
sick days and, 72
low blood sugar. See also hypoglycemia
danger of prolonged periods
without food, 135–138
in middle of night, 38–39
not timing meal with insulin,
19–22

M

managed care
concerns about, 148, 152, 153
Sunshine Laws, 155
meals
delayed, 102–104
Humalog before meals and NPH
insulin in a.m., 34
meat
low-fat, 96
Medical Recovery Services, 157
medical tests
that require prolonged periods
without food, 136–137
Medicare, 153–154

medicine
sugar-free, 79, 82
to stop vomiting, 78
monitoring
basic facts of, 52
blood pressure, 52
blood sugar tests, 43–48
cholesterol, 52
eyes, 51–52
feet, 52
glycosylated hemoglobin, 49–51
urine microalbumin test, 51
urine sugar testing, 48–49
monounsaturated fats, 97

N

National Organization of Physicians
Who Care, 153, 157
NPH insulin, 18
activity of, 24
adjusting to increase flexibility in
dinner time, 102
high blood sugar guidelines, 25
Humalog before meals and NPH
insulin in a.m., 34
low blood sugar guidelines, 26
nutrition. See also ingredient list
airplane food, 111
amount of food to consume,
33–34
artificial sweeteners, 95–96
basic needs of, 30
basic tips for, 40
bedtime snacks, 36, 38–39
carbohydrate counting, 89
carbohydrate intake and insulin
dose, 36–37
carbohydrates combined with
protein and fat, 32–33
dietetic foods, 98
dividing up food throughout the
day, 34
fats, 96–98
Humalog before meals and NPH
insulin in a.m., 34
limiting refined sugar, 89
on sick days, 76–77
sugar and sweets in, 31–32
timing insulin with eating, 37–38
withholding food and danger of,
134–138

Nutrition Facts label
  serving size, 93
  Total Carbohydrates, 93

━━━ P

pain/fever medication
  sugar-free, 82
pancreas
  artificial, 189
pancreatic transplants, 188
Patient Advocacy Coalition, 157
patient advocacy organizations,
  156–157
peanut butter, 90–91
polyunsaturated fats, 97
pop
  hypoglycemia and, 58, 65
  times you can have, 91
preferred provider organization, 162

━━━ R

red blood cells
  glycosylation of, 50–51
refined sugar
  avoiding, 31–32
  high sugar ingredients, 90, 92
  ingredient list and, 90, 92
  limiting, 88–89
  rules for identifying high-sugar
    foods, 92
Regular insulin, 17–18
  activity of, 24
  high blood sugar guidelines, 25
  low blood sugar guidelines, 26
  snacks and, 21
  timing with eating food, 19–21
relatives of persons with diabetes
  immunologic tests for, 183–187
research
  for stopping diabetes, 187
  immunologic tests and, 183–187
  insulin-pump, 189
  pancreatic transplants, 188
  vaccine for diabetes, 188
retinopathy, 52

━━━ S

same-day surgery, 131–138
  danger of prolonged period with-
    out food, 135–136
  Type 1 compared to Type 2
    diabetes, 134

saturated fats, 96, 97
short-acting insulin, 17–18
sick days, 69–83
  blood sugar testing on, 79
  contact with doctor during, 73,
    74, 83
  diabetic ketoacidosis and, 71–72
  fluid intake on, 77–78
  foods for, 76–77
  insulin amount taken during, 72,
    74
  insulin supplements for, 75
  steps for care on, 74
  summary guide for, 83
  supplies to stock before, 78–79
  urine testing and, 79
single-voided urine test, 79–80
snacks
  bedtime, 36, 38–39
  Regular insulin and, 21
Society for Education of Physicians
  and Patients, 157
static dosing
  drawbacks of, 16
stress, 141–145
  blood sugar level and, 141–144
  hormones and, 142–143
  tips for minimizing, 145
sugar. See also refined sugar; sweets
  high sugar ingredients, 90, 92
  rules for identifying high-sugar
    foods, 92
sugar-free medicines, 79, 82
Sunshine Laws, 155
sweets. See also refined sugar; sugar
  avoiding, 31–32

━━━ T

thirst, 5
Tigan suppositories, 78
time zones
  changes in, and insulin adjust
    ments, 110, 113–114
Transderm Scopalamine patch, 78
travel, 109–117
  airplane food, 111
  airplane tips for, 111–112
  back-up supply of insulin, 109–110
  hand-carried bag for, 111, 117
  insulin adjustments for time zone
    changes, 110, 113–114

out-of-country travel tips, 112,
115
preparing for medical care, 113,
116
summary of tips for, 117
Type 1 diabetes
alcohol and, 104–106
characteristics of, 10
defined, 10
same-day surgery, 134
urine ketone testing, 48
Type 2 diabetes
alcohol and, 104–106
characteristics of, 10
defined, 10
same-day surgery, 134
treatment for, 11
urine ketone testing, 48–49

━━ U
unconscious state
diabetes identification and, 64, 66
glucagon and, 63
hypoglycemia and, 63
preparation in advance for, 64, 66
upper GI, 136
urine testing
double-voided, 79–80
microalbumin test, 51
morning test for sugar and
ketone, 53
reason for, 48
sick days and, 79
single-voided, 79–80

━━ V
vaccine for diabetes, 188
vomiting, 74
medicine to stop, 78

━━ W
weight loss, 5
dieting, 172–173